T0158920

Where does your favorite Hall of Famer rank?

SAWS

SEASON ADJUSTED WINS ABOVE REPLACEMENT SCORE

A New Way of Ranking Baseball Players in the Hall of Fame

BOB GLIDEWELL

authorHOUSE®

AuthorHouse™
1663 Liberty Drive
Bloomington, IN 47403
www.authorhouse.com
Phone: 1 (800) 839-8640

Published by AuthorHouse 06/27/2018

ISBN: 978-1-5462-4338-0 (sc)
ISBN: 978-1-5462-4337-3 (e)

Library of Congress Control Number: 2018906054

Print information available on the last page.

Contents

INTRODUCTION

INTRODUCTION

There is a concept with which many baseball fans are familiar known as Wins Above Replacement (WAR). Organizations, including Baseball-Reference.com and SABR, Society for American Baseball Research, a group of which I am a member, have discussed or revised this concept for many years. The purpose of it is to rank baseball players according to how many wins, via runs, they produce over and above that which the hypothetical player who would replace them would produce. I think it is beautiful and I have no desire to analyze its methodology for any more suggestions as to revision.

The original rankings were simply based on the total number of Wins Above Replacement the player produced during his career determined by simply adding the wins of each year. Then along came Jay Jaffe and added a new twist to the formula. He suggested that you determine the seven best WAR years or "peak" of each player and average that cumulative figure in with the total figure. This was the recognition of quality in addition to the quantity of WAR. He called it JAWS for Jaffe Wins Above Replacement Score and uses it for determination of Hall of Fame rankings and how a player compares to the average JAWS score of a Hall of Famer. His Hall of Fame rankings were by position where the player generated the most value and not necessarily the most games played. This new process helped players with fewer years but stellar years to rise in the rankings.

In reviewing the moves in rank a player could make using JAWS instead of WAR I was somewhat disappointed. Only occasionally did JAWS move a player even two slots up in their positional rankings and rarely did it move the player three or more spots. It did have a greater effect if you consolidated all position players. Jackie Robinson lost approximately half of a major league career due to discrimination and ended up with only ten seasons; Hank Greenberg lost almost four years to military service and managed thirteen total seasons with only eleven full seasons; Ralph Kiner could only amass ten seasons before his back injuries sidelined him permanently. Using only Hall of Fame players (excluding Negro League players and players elected as managers or pioneers) for ranking, Jackie Robinson had a WAR rank of 83rd and a JAWS rank of 62nd. But his movement within second basemen was only from eleventh to ninth. Hank Greenberg barely moved from 89th under WAR to 80th under JAWS while only moving from fourteenth to twelfth in the first base category. Ralph Kiner went from 118th in JAWS to 96th for all Hall of Famers but only from sixteenth to fourteenth in the left field room.

Then I discovered more. Joe DiMaggio, Sandy Koufax, Dan Brouthers, Billy Hamilton, Buck Ewing, Roger Bresnahan, Hughie Jennings, Larry Doby, Earle Combs, Sam Thompson, Frank Chance, Mickey Cochrane, Whitey Ford, Dizzy Dean, Rube Waddell, Pedro Martinez and Elmer Flick just to name a few. Check out Johan Santana and his short career for Hall of Fame snubs. All seem to be afflicted by the fewer number of seasons played or the fewer number of games in a season for those playing in the 19th century. It was becoming obvious to me that shorter careers (10-15 years) were not regarded as qualifying for the Hall as easily and quickly as longer careers (15-20 years). They sure did not receive the respect of the longer careers in voting numbers either. It crosses my mind more than occasionally that if more quantity than ten years of play was required of Hall of Fame candidates the Hall of Fame would have put the requirement at more than ten years. Effectively the writers seem to have.

It also seemed to me that a low common denominator was needed to level the playing field between longer and shorter careers. Comparing a player with 14 seasons and a player with 22 seasons seemed to be the proverbial comparison of apples and oranges. Comparing players by averaging WAR by number of seasons did not lend itself to equality since one player could play 162 games within a season and another could play 132 games. Games played was my next thought but after quite a bit of number crunching I felt it was still uneven. One player can play all nine innings of a game and another can play only four innings. So now I am down to innings played as a low common denominator. And then I thought I could go even lower with plate appearances, but plate appearances relate only to offensive numbers whereas WAR, and consequently JAWS, all have defensive factors included in the calculations. So, innings played was as my lowest common denominator.

It would be simple. Determine from innings played how many "effective seasons" each player has. First, divide total innings played by nine and that gives you total number of nine inning games played in a career. Then divide that figure by 162 and you have the total number of effective seasons. Or for a one step calculation you could simply divide the total innings played by 1458 innings which is nine times 162.

For pitchers I decided on 250 innings for an effective year of a starter. Using today's standards an ace of the staff might get 35 starts and pitch seven innings of each start. That computes to 245 innings so I just rounded to 250. Looking at relief pitchers' statistics for innings pitched I just estimated 100 innings as an effective year for them.

Once I had effective years for a player I could divide that figure into whatever figure I wanted including WAR, Offensive WAR, (oWAR), Defensive WAR, (dWAR), home runs, runs batted in and so on and so on. Every player's production is based upon the same standard – a per year calculation. I simply called it Season Adjusted Wins Above Replacement Score or SAWS.

The final thing I had to decide is how to analyze my rankings. As a college professor in the second half of my career I choose to grade "on the curve." This means that you must score

60% of the highest score to pass the test or class. That is one option I have noted. The other is to use the median. If you cannot perform in the top half of the room, you probably should not be there. Averages are fine but one or two high or low scores can skew an average.

It would be very easy at this point to come up with clichés to justify my thinking. Things like bigger is not necessarily better, quantity does not always indicate quality or something even more abstract like "less is more" could at least rationalize my endeavor. SAWS is not perfect. It does tend to reward, or at least compensate for, shorter careers and penalize those who hang on. It is essentially a calculation of an average and more years with fewer Wins Above Replacement tend to lower the overall average just like a .237 BA in your last year can lower your career BA below the magical mark of .300. Think: Mickey Mantle. But then again WAR was penalizing shorter careers and JAWS was not picking up enough slack for me.

Let me make it clear at this point. If I am a major league ball player getting paid tons of money to play a children's game I am going to hang on as long as I can. You will have to arrest me and put me in shackles to get me out of the ballpark. I really could not care less that some numbers cruncher comes along years later and says it hurts my all-time ranking.

SAWS is in no way intended to replace or in any way malign WAR or JAWS. It is simply another way of valuing baseball players. It stresses quality over quantity. Besides, no one singular number is a tell all, save all, be all, end all to the argument of who is the best. There are so many intangibles to a player's career to qualify him for the Hall that I won't even try to list them. Nor do I wish to get bogged down by them. And some major things like MVP or All-Star selections or awards like Cy Young, Rookie of the Year and Gold Glove still have an element of popularity in them. They will, though, be used extensively with comments on each player.

Let's talk for a moment about how a player gets into the Hall of Fame. Without parsing all the rules, he can be elected by the Baseball Writers Association of America (BBWAA). Currently each qualifying writer can vote for up to ten eligible players on any yearly ballot. And there has always been an Old Timers or Veterans Committee, now known as Era Committees, for those who never made admission by being named on 75% of the writers' ballots. If you want someone to blame for players you think should not be in the Hall then pick one of those two. I could gripe endlessly about some of the selections by both and could gripe even more about the current votes being so liberally tossed around by the writers. Too many players are receiving a higher percentage of the votes than the "Five Immortals" elected in 1936. Cobb, Ruth, Wagner, Johnson and Mathewson are still at the top of most lists.

Consider the following:

From 1937 through 1962 inclusive (26 years) only one player received more than 90% of the votes. That was Bob Feller, the Cleveland Indians' legendary fire-baller. From 1963 through

1988 (26 years) only six inductees received 90% or more of the votes. They were Ted Williams, Stan Musial, Willie Mays, Hank Aaron and Brooks Robinson. Some names, huh? The sixth was Luke Appling who got 70% in a nominating vote in 1964 and since no one garnered 75% of the votes a run-off was held whereby one player with the highest number of votes won induction. From 1989 through 2015 (27 years) a total of 20 inductees have surpassed the 90% mark. Four inductees – Tom Seaver, Nolan Ryan, George Brett and Cal Ripken – have tied or exceeded the 98.2% received by Ty Cobb. Six more have received a higher percentage of the votes than Babe Ruth! In 2016 we have Ken Griffey, in my opinion, a player with an overall record not all that close in comparison to other centerfielders and renowned home run hitters in the Hall (and I will vigorously defend that statement later), elected by the highest percentage ever, 99.3%. Following him in 2018 is Chipper Jones with another 98.2%. I have nothing personally against these players, but I reserve the right to address their statistical quality or comparison, as I have analyzed it, for Hall status and will do so later in this writing. I am suggesting that current baseball writers and Veterans committees have little or no regard for the past and little or no comparative insights. I will grant you than I have access to far more information and mathematical formulae than earlier writers and voters but the existence of all that math and information sure doesn't seem to be used. You can argue that a certain player is going to eventually go into the Hall no matter what one writer's vote will be, so you might as well go ahead and vote for him now. That may be true and hold some logic. Take George Brett for instance. Clearly, he deserves the Hall of Fame and clearly, he is the greatest Kansas City Royal to date. I lived in Kansas City in the early Eighties and got to see him play. But does he deserve a first ballot vote percentage greater than Babe Ruth? Read my discussion of him in Third Basemen.

What also amazes me is how some players start with a few percentage points of votes in their first ballot year and then somehow miraculously rise to 75 % over many years of votes. Somewhere in this world there is an explanation for that phenomenon. I just do not know what it is.

One pet peeve I have concerns comments I have read on the internet that baseball writers who return a blank ballot should be disqualified from future voting. Why? It is every bit possible that no one on the ballot qualifies or will ever be elected so why penalize someone for not voting for a slate of unqualified candidates? Sometimes I also think that the committees must have felt obligated to choose someone to prove their worth. I could consider who some committees voted for as the reason to end that committee.

The question really becomes: how many people do you want in the Hall of Fame? As of this writing there have been 323, 226 of which are players other than Negro Leaguers, selected since the first vote in 1936. That is almost four per year and in 2018 four were elected by the writers and two by a committee. In 82 more years you could be looking at 646 and those elected might begin to feel it is not such an honor. The fans may then consider the Hall of Fame to be a joke, if some don't feel that way already.

Another point to consider is the first writers selected five players from the first sixty-five years of organized professional baseball. Count'em…five. That's all they thought was worthy of enshrinement.

Some of the basic statistics that get a player into the Hall of Fame are batting average, home runs and hits. A BA of .300 is not even close to a certainty for enshrinement. As of this writing 205 players have hit over .300 and only 157 position players are in the Hall and they do not all have batting averages over .300. 500 home runs are still somewhat of a standard, but that figure was sullied by users of performance enhancing drugs. As for those drug users I shun all of them whether the evidence is direct or circumstantial, proven or just alleged. I think you hurt the game more than you hurt yourself. But it will survive your despicable actions. 3000 hits seem to be the most certain way to get in – not that it should be. Only Pete Rose has achieved that plateau without being enshrined and we all know why. Keep him out.

300 wins for a pitcher is (was?) a sure bet as well but not always on the first ballot. 300 wins is not a sure bet with me as you will see. In fact, seven of the 300 game winners in the Hall were passed over by the writers and chosen by a committee. Three had to wait until a later ballot, as late as the fifth ballot. This is undoubtedly of no concern any longer since I don't think there will ever be a 300-game winner again.

A few personal notes about positions within the Hall. I am not in favor of designated hitters (DH) being in the Hall. Frank Thomas, Paul Molitor and Jim Thome are all in the Hall when they were substantially designated hitters although they are still listed as a position player. David Ortiz will be up for election soon and Edgar Martinez is currently knocking at the door. Designated hitters are not complete ball players. Some are such poor fielders that they could literally cost their team a few games each year. Some are injury prone and would not last playing every day in the field and would have never been carried by a team fifty to sixty years ago, i.e., pre - DH.

My second gripe about the DH position is how many players reached 3000 hits thanks to being a DH. Try Al Kaline, George Brett, Carl Yastrzemski, and maybe even Rod Carew. I wonder how many National Leaguers will come close but not succeed because their bodies give out earlier from playing in the field every day. Is that fair? Or does anyone really consider that?

A special note about DH games and effective seasons. They are each counted as a full game for effective season purposes and that hurts a lot of sluggers who hang on.

The next personal note is about the relief pitcher position. As you will see the concept of WAR, JAWS and even SAWS really is meaningless for relief pitchers. Their numbers pale in comparison to starting pitchers. Recently elected Trevor Hoffman is the worthiest of the six and Mariano Rivera will skate in as he should. I am warming to that position much more so than DH.

There are players that have above average and above median statistics that are about as exciting as off-white wall paint. Addressing each player leads to boring repetition sometimes. Before the final calculations and the first draft of this manuscript I also read what I could find on each Hall of Fame inductee including, and especially, the Player Bios from SABR BioProject before finalizing this manuscript. I plan to stick with numbers and use very little of those writings, but I strongly recommend reading them. Most players have a moderate to good argument for being the Hall but not always a winning argument. Most arguments do not even mention any negatives. So many of them really do not impress or make an impact or contribute that certain something that makes you remember them or makes them great or *famous.* Remember it is called a Hall of *Fame.*

ABBREVIATIONS AND CATEGORIES OF COMPARISON

All statistics have been extracted from the Baseball-Reference.com website with their permission. Data is subject to change without notice.

Many abbreviations for position player statistics that I use are as follows:

BA = Batting Average

OBP = On Base Percentage

SLG = Slugging Percentage

OPS = On Base Plus Slugging Percentage

OPS+ = OPS Adjusted for the league and park

oWAR = Offensive Wins Above Replacement

dWAR = Defensive Wins Above Replacement

SO/BB = Strikeout to Base on Ball Ratio

DP = Double Plays

FP = Fielding Percentage

RF = Range Factor

DH = Designated Hitter

CS = Caught Stealing

/162 means season adjusted to 162 nine inning games or per effective season

C = Catcher; SP = Starting Pitcher; RP = Relief Pitcher; 1B = First Base; 2B = Second Base; SS = Shortstop; 3B = Third Base; LF = Left Field; CF = Centerfield; RF = Right Field.

All positions except pitchers will reflect actual seasons, effective seasons and effective seasons at the specific position. Pitchers will not have effective seasons at pitcher.

Catcher will have special defensive categories of caught stealing - percentage above league caught stealing rate and season adjusted passed balls.

Infielders will have categories of season adjusted assists, errors and double plays. First Basemen will not have double plays listed.

Second basemen and shortstops will have season adjusted steals as those are the two positions which have the most players with over 300 steals.

All positions players will have traditional slash statistics including batting average, on base percentage, slugging percentage and on base plus slugging. OPS+ will not be listed for second basemen and shortstops. Strikeout to base on ball ratio will be listed for all position players. All position players will reflect home runs, runs batted in, runs scored and runs created and all will be season adjusted.

All positions except catcher will reflect Player Fielding Percentage compared to League Fielding Percentage. Those numbers will be listed from highest actual fielding percentage to lowest actual fielding percentage. A high FP may actually be below league average and low percentage may actually be way above league average. Be careful that you note that.

Range factor is noted as the number of plays above or below league average for an effective season.

League leaderships are only for six main batting categories of BA, OBP, SLG, OPS, HR and RBI.

For Starting Pitchers:

SHO = Shutouts

SO = Strikeouts

WP = Wild Pitches.

ERA = Earned Run Average

ERA+ = Earned Run Average adjusted for the league and park

WHIP = Walks and Hits per Inning Pitched

W/L% = Won – Loss Percentage

/162 means season adjusted to 162 nine inning games or per effective season

All pitchers will have traditional statistics of wins, won-loss percentage, ERA and adjusted ERA. Non-traditional statistics will include season adjusted wins, shutouts, strikeouts.

Relief Pitchers will have the standard categories of SAWS, JAWS and WAR but other specific categories will be suggested for your review.

Defensive comparisons only use the number of innings played at the position for which they have been assigned by JAWS. In the case of outfielders, specific information about innings per position is not available so total outfield innings are used.

Dominance rankings can be found in the last section entitled Position Player Consolidations. For position players and starting pitchers their league leaderships in the respective three Triple Crown categories are divided by effective seasons and converted to what is actually season adjusted league leaderships.

The reader must recognize that certain figures and comparisons, both defensive and offensive, will be greatly affected by the era in which was played. All fans know about the lack of gloves in the original years of baseball which greatly affected defense; and they know about the "dead ball" era and the "live ball" era which greatly affected offense. Rule changes such as moving the pitchers' box/mound back to 60" 6" or lowering the mound from 15 inches to 10 inches also had an effect on pitching. The DH is ever present with American League players. Sometimes all you can do is compare players within each era as best you can.

This analysis only compares some the statistics that can be reduced to a seasonal adjustment. Obviously other statistics may be considered by some as more important than the ones I have used but I try to stick with major categories.

I will offer brief commentary about all the players within each position, ranked according to SAWS, as well as a few overlooked and upcoming candidates, but I will again stress that my opinions are not the point of this writing. I will also keep my comments centered around a player's complete record and try to stay away from the minutia or cherry-picked qualifications. The only calculated numbers I wish to use are WAR, JAWS, oWAR, dWAR and runs created. The rest are traditional numbers. I believe in the "KISS" theory for practically everything. Keep it short and simple. Besides, the SAWS calculations are the crux, not the commentary as it is pure opinion. And besides, some of my comments are very terse and more than a little edgy in places. Some are simply repetitive and boring especially with the pitchers. You will quickly see that I think the Hall is overcrowded and getting worse. If I could "un-induct" some I would.

CATCHERS

THE SEASONS

	Actual	Total Effective	Effective Seasons at C
1.	Carlton Fisk – 24	14.0738	12.6963
2.	Ivan Rodriguez – 21	14.3477	13.9561
3.	Gabby Hartnett – 20	10.5048	10.3182
4.	Yogi Berra – 19	11.3116	9.8395
5.	Gary Carter – 19	12.9726	11.9129
6.	Buck Ewing – 18	7.7596	3.7119
7.	Rick Ferrell – 18	10.3882	10.3882
8.	Ray Schalk – 18	9.8663	9.8663
9.	Johnny Bench – 17	12.1488	9.9370
10.	Bill Dickey – 17	9.8635	9.8635
11.	Ernie Lombardi – 17	8.6722	8.6722
12.	Roger Bresnahan – 17	7.6694	5.4746
13.	Mike Piazza – 16	10.4065	9.2970
14.	Mickey Cochrane – 13	8.2490	8.2455
15.	Roy Campanella – 10	6.9472	6.9472

THE RANKINGS

Here are the SAWS, WAR and JAWS ranking and scores for each player.

	SAWS	WAR	JAWS
1.	Mickey Cochrane – 6.32	Bench – 75.2	Bench – 61.2
2.	Johnny Bench – 6.19	Carter – 70.1	Carter – 59.3
3.	Buck Ewing – 6.12	Rodriguez – 68.7	Rodriquez – 54.3
4.	Mike Piazza – 5.71	Fisk – 68.5	Fisk – 53.0
5.	Bill Dickey – 5.66	Piazza – 59.6	Piazza – 51.4
6.	Gary Carter – 5.40	Berra – 59.4	Berra – 48.2
7.	Roger Bresnahan – 5.33	Dickey – 55.8	Dickey – 45.0
8.	Ernie Lombardi – 5.29	Hartnett – 53.4	Cochrane – 44.5
9.	Yogi Berra – 5.25	Cochrane – 52.1	Hartnett – 41.9
10.	Gabby Hartnett – 5.07	Ewing – 47.7	Ewing – 39.1
11.	Roy Campanella – 4.91	Lombardi – 45.9	Lombardi – 36.9
12.	Carlton Fisk – 4.87	Bresnahan – 40.9	Bresnahan – 34.9
13.	Ivan Rodriguez – 4.77	Campanella – 34.1	Campanella – 33.5
14.	Ray Schalk – 2.89	Ferrell – 29.8	Schalk – 25.3
15.	Rick Ferrell – 2.87	Schalk – 28.6	Ferrell – 24.8

THE OFFENSIVE COMPARISONS

	BA	OBP	SLG	OPS
1.	Cochrane - .320	Cochrane - .419	Piazza - .545	Piazza - .922
2.	Dickey - .313	Bresnahan - .386	Campanella - .500	Cochrane - .897
3.	Piazza - .308	Dickey - .382	Dickey - .492	Dickey - .868
4.	Lombardi - .306	Ferrell - .378	Hartnett - .489	Campanella - .860
5.	Ewing - .303	Piazza - .377	Berra - .482	Hartnett - .858
6.	Hartnett - .297	Hartnett - .370	Cochrane - .478	Berra - .830
7.	Rodriquez - .296	Campanella - .360	Bench - .476	Lombardi - .818
8.	Berra - .285	Lombardi - .358	Rodriguez - .464	Bench - .817
9.	Ferrell - .281	Ewing - .351	Lombardi - .460	Ewing - .807
10.	Bresnahan - .279	Berra - .348	Fisk - .457	Rodriguez - .798
11.	Campanella - .276	Bench - .342	Carter - .439	Fisk - .797
12.	Fisk - .269	Fisk - .341	Ewing - .406	Carter - .773
13.	Bench - .267	Schalk - .340	Bresnahan - .377	Bresnahan - .764
14.	Carter - .262	Carter - .335	Ferrell - .363	Ferrell - .747
15.	Schalk - .253	Rodriquez - .334	Schalk - .316	Schalk - .656

	oWAR/162	Runs Created/162	SO/BB Ratio	OPS+
1.	Piazza – 6.38	Piazza – 132.42	Cochrane - .250	Piazza - 142
2.	Cochrane – 6.35	Cochrane – 124.01	Ferrell - .305	Cochrane - 129
3.	Lombardi – 5.59	Dickey – 118.01	Dickey - .426	Ewing - 129
4.	Bresnahan – 5.58	Berra – 111.83	Schalk - .561	Berra - 127
5.	Dickey – 5.46	Ewing – 110.96	Bresnahan - .564	Dickey - 127
6.	Ewing – 5.45	Hartnett – 110.52	Berra - .588	Lombardi - 127
7.	Bench – 5.42	Lombardi – 110.47	Lombardi - .609	Bench - 226
8.	Hartnett – 5.02	Campanella – 108.96	Ewing - .750	Bresnahan - 126
9.	Berra – 5.01	Bench – 101.99	Campanella - .940	Hartnett - 126
10.	Campanella – 4.87	Fisk – 97.91	Hartnett - .991	Campanella - 123
11.	Fisk – 4.71	Rodriguez – 97.44	Carter - 1.176	Fisk - 117
12.	Carter – 4.34	Carter – 91.27	Bench - 1.434	Carter - 115
13.	Rodriguez – 3.80	Bresnahan – 84.49	Piazza - 1.466	Rodriguez - 106
14.	Ferrell – 2.93	Ferrell – 79.51	Fisk – 1.632	Ferrell - 95
15.	Schalk – 2.41	Schalk – NA(1)	Rodriguez – 2.873	Schalk – 83

(1) Ray Schalk was not in the top 1000 players under Leaders – Runs Created in Baseball-Reference.com. The lowest player listed when research was done had 592 career runs created. Therefore, since Schalk played 9.8663 effective seasons his runs created per season had to be less than 60.0022.

	Home Runs/162	Runs Batted In/162	Runs Scored/162
1.	Piazza – 41.03	Piazza – 128.29	Ewing – 144.83
2.	Campanella – 34.83	Berra – 126.42	Cochrane – 126.20
3.	Bench – 32.02	Campanella – 123.22	Berra – 103.88
4.	Berra – 31.65	Dickey – 122.57	Piazza – 100.71
5.	Fisk – 26.72	Lombardi – 114.15	Rodriguez – 94.37
6.	Carter – 24.88	Ewing – 113.27	Dickey – 94.29
7.	Hartnett – 22.47	Bench – 113.26	Fisk – 90.66
8.	Lombardi – 21.91	Hartnett – 112.23	Campanella – 90.25
9.	Rodriguez – 21.68	Cochrane – 100.62	Bench – 89.80
10.	Dickey – 20.48	Fisk – 94.50	Bresnahan – 88.92
11.	Cochrane – 14.43	Carter – 94.43	Hartnett – 82.53
12.	Ewing – 9.11	Rodriguez – 92.84	Carter – 79.01
13.	Bresnahan – 3.39	Ferrell – 70.66	Lombardi – 69.30
14.	Ferrell – 2.70	Bresnahan – 67.11	Ferrell – 66.13
15.	Schalk – 1.11	Schalk – 60.10	Schalk – 58.68

THE DEFENSIVE COMPARISONS

	Assists/162	Errors/162	Double Plays/162
1.	Ewing – 273.78	Bench – 9.76	Schalk – 22.50
2.	Bresnahan – 218.28	Carter – 10.16	Ewing – 21.01
3.	Schalk – 183.56	Rodriguez – 10.25	Berra – 17.79
4.	Hartnett – 121.53	Dickey – 10.95	Bresnahan – 17.54
5.	Ferrell – 108.49	Berra – 11.18	Hartnett – 15.80
6.	Cochrane – 101.78	Fisk – 12.21	Dickey – 13.89
7.	Carter – 100.98	Campanella – 12.24	Ferrell – 13.38
8.	Lombardi – 97.44	Ferrell – 12.99	Bench – 12.78
9.	Dickey – 96.72	Piazza – 13.33	Cochrane – 12.61
10.	Rodriguez – 87.92	Cochrane – 13.46	Carter – 12.51
11.	Bench – 85.54	Hartnett – 13.47	Lombardi – 12.34
12.	Fisk – 82.54	Lombardi – 16.49	Campanella – 11.80
13.	Berra – 81.11	Schalk – 17.74	Fisk – 11.58
14.	Campanella – 79.17	Bresnahan – 30.50	Rodriguez – 11.32
15.	Piazza – 78.84	Ewing – 86.75	Piazza – 9.47

	Passed Balls/162	CS - % Above League	dWAR/162
1.	Carter – 7.05	Rodriguez: + 48.39%	Rodriguez – 2.06
2.	Dickey – 7.71	Campanella: + 35.71%	Carter – 2.01

3. Berra – 7.724	Hartnett: + 27.27%	Bench – 1.62
4. Campanella – 8.06	Bench: + 22.86%	Schalk – 1.39
5. Rodriguez – 9.17	Schalk: + 15.91%	Fisk – 1.208
6. Bench – 9.46	Dickey: + 14.63%	Ewing – 1.21
7. Schalk – 9.83	Carter: + 9.38%	Campanella - .82
8. Fisk – 10.16	Berra: + 8.89%	Berra - .778
9. Cochrane – 10.67	Ferrell: + 7.32%	Dickey - .771
10. Piazza – 10.97	Lombardi: + 6.67%	Bresnahan - .64
11. Hartnett – 12.21	Ewing: + 2.7%	Hartnett - .63
12. Ferrell – 13.67	Bresnahan: - 2.22	Cochrane - .53
13. Lombardi – 17.53	Fisk: - 2.86%	Ferrell - .529
14. Bresnahan – 23.56	Cochrane: - 7.14%	Lombardi - .33
15. Ewing – 96.99	Piazza: - 25.81%	Piazza - .14

OBSERVATIONS AND COMMENTARY

Noticeable moves from JAWS to SAWS:

Mickey Cochrane goes from 8th to 1st
Johnny Bench falls from 1st to 2nd
Buck Ewing goes from 10th to 3rd
Roger Bresnahan goes from last to 7th
Carlton Fisk falls from 4rd to 12th
Ivan Rodriquez falls from 3rd to 13th
Gary Carter falls from 2nd to 6th

All but two of the players stay within 60% of the highest score. The median is Ernie Lombardi at 5.29. That would be a debatable cutoff as well.

1. <u>Mickey Cochrane – 1925-1937, WAR 9th, JAWS 8th</u>

   The first thing to notice is the thirteen-year career which usually benefits a player under SAWS but not under WAR or JAWS. Granted his career ended abruptly which eliminates the lowering effect of those last few years, but this is the record we must analyze. Cochrane almost reigns supreme in offensive comparative statistics as he is first in BA, OBP and SO/BB ratio. He is second in OPS, OPS+, runs scored, runs created, OPS, and season adjusted oWAR. He was ahead of Johnny Bench in every category except home runs and runs batted it. He even bested Bench in SLG. He was weaker in defensive comparisons as his placements ran from sixth to fourteenth place. He did receive two All-Star appointments after they began in 1933 and corralled two MVPs. He hit five homers and drove in seven runs in five World Series. The BBWAA was a tough crowd to please in his day and it took him six ballots to round up 79.5% of the vote.

2. Johnny Bench – 1967-1983, WAR 1st, JAWS 1st

Not declaring Johnny Bench first may be likened to heresy or treason or some other sin or violation of the law. But this is a quality versus quantity issue. Bench is not without a strong argument as he won two MVPs, ten Gold Gloves, Rookie of the Year, and received fourteen All-Star appointments and one World Series MVP. But the only comparative category he wins is on defense and that was season adjusted errors at 9.76. He was seventh in oWAR and even third in season adjusted home runs. Otherwise he ranged from seventh to thirteenth in offensive comparisons. He was third in overall dWAR with a fourth-place ranking in caught stealing percentage over league as his second-best category. Still, he strolled into the Hall with a first ballot, 96.4%. I am not arguing his value, just presenting a different ranking system.

3. Buck Ewing – 1880-1897, WAR 10th, JAWS 10th

I can only imagine that very few saw this one coming. Especially since Ewing only played 3.7119 years as a catcher and did so in the nineteenth century. The first Veterans Committee of 1936 showed some respect with 50.6% and the 1939 Old Timers Committee chose him. Apparently those two groups saw some definite value that most people today would not even know about. He was sixth in both oWAR and dWAR. He is tied for second in OPS+ with a 129 and was tied for first until Piazza came along so you know he had strong offensive skills. He was third in BA and fifth in runs created. I know that the era was completely different for style of play, but he does lead the way with runs scored and is second in season adjusted double plays. He also had a .931 fielding percentage to a league rate of .905 so he was a good fielding catcher for his day. SAWS just give us a chance to recognize his abilities.

4. Mike Piazza – 1992-2007, WAR 5th, JAWS 5th

Rumors of performance enhancing drugs (PEDs) were cast aside by the voters when Piazza gained admission with 83% on his fourth ballot. Either that or writers decided that terrible fielding ability should not keep catchers outside of the Hall. Defensively he was last in assists, double plays, caught stealing percentage and dWAR. Offensively I need not repeat what you can see above as he was first in seven offensive categories and first overall in oWAR. He also had nine Silver Sluggers, twelve All-Star appointments, the Rookie of the Year award and climbed to second in one MVP vote. The bad defense alone would have kept him out with me but the PED possibilities sewed it up.

5. Bill Dickey – 1928-1946, WAR 7th, JAWS 7th

   Dickey had better than above average comparison rankings. Defensively he was second lowest in passed balls and fourth lowest in errors and slightly below median in dWAR at ninth. Offensively he was second highest in BA and third highest is OBP, SLG, OPS, runs created and strikeout to base on ball ratio. He was also fourth highest in runs batted in. Overall, he was fifth in oWAR. He was elected to eleven All-Star teams and hit five homers and drove in 25 runs in eight World Series. Remarkably he was not elected until the twelfth ballot with only 80.2% of the vote. I think writers of that era were almost too discriminating.

6. Gary Carter – 1974-1992, WAR 2nd, JAWS 2nd

   Offensively Carter ranked sixth in home runs and didn't rank above eleventh in any other offensive comparison category, so he comes in twelfth in oWAR. Defensively he was first in passed balls and second in errors and second in career and season adjusted dWAR. He also boasted three Gold Gloves, five Silver Sluggers, eleven All-Star teams and two All-Star MVPs. He wasn't elected until his sixth ballot and only with 78% of the vote. He still seems to have what it takes to be a Hall of Famer…but just barely.

7. Roger Bresnahan – 1897-1915, WAR 12th, JAWS 12th

   Joan M. Thomas in her SABR BioProject says that Bresnahan is regarded as the "Deadball Era's most famous catcher as well known for his innovations in protective equipment…" Maybe so. But his numbers don't point to a high probability of being a true Hall of Famer. Offensively all he had was a good OBP, so I don't really know where the good season adjusted oWAR of fourth comes from. In four offensive categories he ranked thirteenth and in one he ranked fourteenth. Defensively he was rather weak with a tenth place in dWAR so the innovations, whatever they may have been, really did not elevate him all that much. He was second in assists and fourth in double plays, though. He did not have much of an arm to throw out runners coming in twelfth with a negative caught stealing rate compared to league. A little more research shows he was a league leader in hit by pitch and base on balls once each. It is getting harder and harder to justify these players based on one calculated number.

8. Ernie Lombardi – 1931-1947, WAR 11th, JAWS 11th

   Lombardi was unmistakably big for a catcher. 6'2" and 220 lbs. was huge, especially for a catcher in 1931. He also has a rarity of league leaderships for a catcher. He led the league in BA twice which helps keep his oWAR up at third which is the best ranking he has offensively. He did come in fourth in BA and fifth in RBI. Otherwise he is middle of the pack. He did rake in one MVP and seven All-Star Games. I am now out of laudatory comments. He is low in the pack defensively and comes in fourteenth out of fifteen in dWAR. His assists come in at eighth, but the rest of the rankings come in below ten. He suffered through twelve ballots before the 1986 Veterans Committee picked him for immortality. This is a tough one to agree with. I really don't.

9. Yogi Berra – 1946-1965, WAR 6th, JAWS 6th

The name alone is Hall of Fame worthy. A second ballot vote of 85.6% is surprising. He is the quintessential image of a major league baseball catcher even more so than Johnny Bench. He is fourth in home runs, second in runs batted in, and third in runs scored. Defensively he is third in double plays and passed balls. So, he is positive in his comparisons but median in his oWAR (9th) and dWAR (8th). He also has three MVPs and fifteen All-Star appointments. Even his "Yogi speak" should be immortalized.

10. Gabby Hartnett – 1922-1941, WAR 8th, JAWS 9th

Hartnett is most well-known for his "homer in the gloamin" hit in 1938 to help his Cubs win a pennant. But a famous home run, as we will also see later, is not the qualifying event for a trip to Cooperstown. Hartnett also picked up one MVP with six All-Star selections, noting when he played and that All-Star games did not begin until 1933. His offensive comparisons are slightly above median to median, but he was fourth in SLG. Defensively he is all over the place but some upper level rankings of third in caught stealing, fourth in assists and fifth in double plays showed up. Overall, he is eighth in oWAR and eleventh in dWAR. It took him thirteen ballots to acquire 77% of the vote. A weak selection.

11. Roy Campanella – 1948-1957, WAR 13th, JAWS 13th

Whether the short career or lingering racism reared its ugly head, this man should not have had to patiently wait through seven ballots before enshrinement. Calculated numbers are not appropriate here. He had three MVPs in ten years. He had the offensive power with home runs, runs batted in and SLG. He had a super arm for nailing runners, second only to Rodriguez and he was fourth in season adjusted passed balls. He had what it takes to be eternally remembered.

12. Carlton Fisk – 1969-1993, WAR 4th, JAWS 4th

He played for a long, long time and built up a lot of WAR and consequently JAWS. But the quality was not necessarily there. Comparative rankings put him from the middle of the pack on down. His dWAR was better than his oWAR, fifth compared to eleventh but he was thirteenth in double plays and caught stealing rate. His rank in homers and runs scored do break into the upper half. Yes, he was chosen for eleven All-Star games but that can be a popularity contest. Yes, he had a game winning home run in the sixth game of the 1975 World Series that will never be forgotten by me. He had a second ballot, 79.6% number. No vote from me.

13. Ivan Rodriquez – 1991-2011, WAR 3rd, JAWS 3rd

Offensively he is clearly in the bottom half of the comparative statistics – he is last in OBP and SO/BB ratio – and comes in thirteenth in oWAR but defensively he is first in dWAR and impressive in his caught stealing above league. He did pull in one MVP, fourteen All-Star games, thirteen Gold Gloves and remarkably, seven Silver Sluggers. What may be more remarkable is that he captured a first ballot prize with 76% of the vote despite the suspicions of PEDs. He would not have received a vote from me.

14. Rick Ferrell – 1929-1947, WAR 14th, JAWS 15th

Ferrell has a few redeeming qualities to be a Hall of Famer. He did get selected to seven All-Star games. His OBP and SO/BB ratio are in the top half of the rankings. The qualities end there. The rest of his rankings are lower half placements. Thanks to Ray Schalk he never reaches last place. He is fourteenth in dWAR and thirteenth in oWAR. The writers gave him all of .5% of the vote in three ballots but the Veterans Committee saw fit to choose him for Cooperstown in 1984. I cannot imagine why and really don't want to know. He is not Hall quality.

15. Ray Schalk – 1912-1929, WAR 15th, JAWS 14th

If any player is a head scratcher it is Schalk. He is at the bottom of the barrel offensively especially with a BA of .253, which, by the way, is the lowest in the Hall. He was last in oWAR. He was last in nine offensive comparisons. He was relatively high in assists and dWAR and plucked out first place in double plays and fourth overall in dWAR but the praise ends there. He was a small catcher and may have had good fielding ability, but he is probably remembered best for not being a cheater in the 1919 World Series. That is admirable but not Hall qualifications.

THE OTHERS

Ted Simmons had a long career in the majors (21 seasons) but only scores 3.7276 in his SAWS which would rank him right above Ray Schalk who is last. His WAR would have put him tenth in the room and his JAWS of 42.4 would have raised him to eighth. With his SAWS that low I see no need to go further.

Thurman Munson clocks in with a 5.9131 SAWS which puts him in fourth position. His WAR of 46.1 places him eleventh and JAWS places him tenth. His dWAR was 1.5264 making him the fourth best defensive catcher. His caught stealing rate was 25.71% better than the league again good for a four slot. A lot of people would look at his short stay of eleven seasons, but Sandy Koufax and Dizzy Dean only had twelve each. His effective years of 7.7963 are greater than Ewing, Bresnahan and Campanella and just a half year behind Cochrane. Munson also batted .292, won Rookie of the Year and one MVP in six considerations and was chosen to seven All-Star games. His voting started at 16.5% and sunk to a low of 4.8% in fifteen ballots. The appropriate Veterans Committee needs to step up when the time comes.

FIRST BASEMEN

THE SEASONS

	Actual	Total Effective	Effective Seasons at 1B
1.	Cap Anson – 27	15.2922	12.8731
2.	Tony Perez – 23	14.9147	9.8409
3.	Harmon Killebrew – 22	13.3535	5.3571
4.	Willie McCovey – 22	12.9616	11.4662
5.	Jim Thome – 22	14.4166	6.5489
6.	Eddie Murray – 21	18.0786	14.5069
7.	Jimmie Foxx – 20	13.0269	11.5055
8.	Jake Beckley – 20	14.3052	14.2812
9.	Dan Brouthers – 19	10.0727	9.8210
10.	Frank Thomas – 19	13.9659	5.7449
11.	Roger Connor – 18	12.1097	10.6029
12.	Lou Gehrig – 17	12.9602	12.9156
13.	Frank Chance – 17	7.2942	5.9575
14.	Orlando Cepeda – 17	12.3006	9.9835
15.	Jim Bottomley – 16	11.3711	11.3690
16.	High Pockets Kelly – 16	9.3676	8.2119
17.	Johnny Mize – 15	9.8599	9.8136
18.	George Sisler – 15	12.275	11.9623
19.	Jeff Bagwell – 15	12.7698	12.7031
20.	Bill Terry – 14	9.6356	9.5645
21.	Hank Greenberg – 13	8.2771	6.8580

THE RANKINGS

	SAWS	WAR	JAWS
1.	Lou Gehrig – 8.67	Gehrig – 112.4	Gehrig – 90.1
2.	Dan Brouthers – 7.92	Foxx – 96.1	Foxx – 77.8
3.	Jimmie Foxx – 7.40	Anson – 94.2	Anson – 68.0
4.	Johnny Mize – 7.20	Connor – 84.3	Connor – 65.6
5.	Roger Connor – 6.961	Bagwell – 79.9	Bagwell – 64.1
6.	Hank Greenberg – 6.959	Brouthers – 79.8	Brouthers – 63.5
7.	Jeff Bagwell – 6.26	Thomas – 73.9	Mize – 59.8
8.	Frank Chance – 6.23	Thome – 72.9	Thomas – 59.6
9.	Cap Anson – 6.14	Mize – 70.9	Thome – 57.2
10.	Bill Terry – 5.61	Murray – 68.7	McCovey – 54.7
11.	Frank Thomas – 5.29	McCovey – 64.5	Murray – 53.9

12. Jim Thome – 5.06	Beckley – 61.6	Greenberg – 52.6
13. Willie McCovey – 4.97	Killebrew – 60.4	Sisler – 50.5
14. Harmon Killebrew – 4.52	Greenberg – 57.6	Killebrew – 49.3
15. George Sisler – 4.40	Terry – 54.2	Terry – 47.7
16. Jake Beckley – 4.30	Sisler – 54.0	Beckeley – 45.7
17. Orlando Cepeda – 4.08	Perez – 54.0	Perez – 45.3
18. Eddie Murray – 3.80	Cepeda – 50.2	Cepeda – 42.4
19. Tony Perez – 3.62	Chance – 45.6	Chance – 40.6
20. Jim Bottomley – 3.10	Bottomley – 35.3	Bottomley – 32.1
21. High Pockets Kelly – 2.70	Kelly – 25.3	Kelly – 24.6

THE OFFENSIVE COMPARISONS

	BA	OBP	SLG	OPS
1.	Brouthers - .342	Gehrig - .447	Gehrig - .632	Gehrig - 1.082
2.	Terry - .341	Foxx - .428	Foxx - .609	Foxx - 1.038
3.	Gehrig - .3401	Brouthers - .423	Greenberg - .605	Greenberg - 1.017
4.	Sisler - .3401	Thomas - .419	Mize - .562	Thomas - .974
5.	Anson - .334	Greenberg - .412	Thomas - .555	Mize - .959
6.	Foxx - .325	Bagwell - .408	Thome - .554	Thome - .956
7.	Connor - .316	Thome - .402	Bagwell - .540	Bagwell - .948
8.	Greenberg - .313	Mize - .3971	Brouthers - .519	Brouthers - .942
9.	Mize - .312	Connor - .3969	McCovey - .515	Terry - .899
10.	Bottomley - .310	Anson - .394	Killebrew - .509	McCovey - .889
11.	Beckley - .308	Chance - .394	Terry - .506	Killebrew - .884
12.	Thomas - .301	Terry - .393	Bottomley - .500	Connor - .883
13.	Bagwell - .2968	Sisler - .379	Cepeda - .499	Bottomley - .869
14.	Kelly - .2967	Killebrew - .376	Connor - .486	Cepeda - .849
15.	Cepeda - .2966	McCovey - .374	Murray - .476	Sisler - .847
16.	Chance - .2963	Bottomley - .369	Sisler - .468	Anson - .841
17.	Murray - .287	Beckley - .361	Perez - .463	Murray - .836
18.	Perez - .279	Murray - .359	Kelly - .452	Perez - .804
19.	Thome - .276	Cepeda - .350	Anson - .447	Beckley - .797
20.	McCovey - .270	Kelly - .342	Beckley - .436	Chance - .788
21.	Killebrew - .256	Perez - .341	Chance - .394	Kelly - .794

	oWAR/162	Runs Created/162	SO/BB Ratio	OPS+
1.	Gehrig – 8.66	Gehrig – 172.30	Brouthers - .283	Gehrig - 179
2.	Brouthers – 8.18	Foxx – 163.51	Anson - .335	Brouthers - 171

3. Foxx – 7.23	Greenberg – 156.09	Connor – .454	Foxx – 163
4. Mize – 7.03	Mize – 145.34	Gehrig – .533	Mize – 158
5. Greenberg – 6.77	Brouthers – 143.95	Chance – .575	Greenburg – 158
6. Connor – 6.56	Thomas – 143.35	Mize – .612	Thomas – 156
7. Anson – 5.99	Bagwell – 140.02	Sisler – .693	Connor – 153
8. Bagwell – 5.86	Thome – 138.10	Terry – .836	Bagwell – 149
9. Thomas – 5.76	Terry – 132.59	Thomas – .838	McCovey – 147
10. McCovey – 5.55	McCovey – 126.37	Beckley – .852	Bagwell – 147
11. Chance – 5.50	Connor – 123.62	Bottomley – .890	Killebrew – 143
12. Thome – 5.38	Bottomley – 121.45	Foxx – .903	Anson – 142
13. Killebrew – 5.36	Killebrew – 120.27	Greenberg – .991	Terry – 136
14. Terry – 4.91	Sisler – 119.59	Killebrew – 1.090	Chance – 135
15. Sisler – 4-35	Anson – 117.97	Bagwell – 1.112	Cepeda – 133
16. Beckley – 4.17	Cepeda – 108.69	Murray – 1.137	Murray – 129
17. Cepeda – 4.10	Murray – 107.42	McCovey – 1.152	Sisler – 125
18. Bottomley – 3.78	Beckley – 102.48	Bagwell – 1.311	Bottomley – 125
19. Murray – 3.44	Perez – 102.18	Kelly – 1.798	Beckley – 125
20. Perez – 3.42	Kelly – 98.32	Cepeda – 1.988	Perez – 122
21. Kelly – 2.23	Chance – 87.88	Perez – 2.018	Kelly – 109

HR/162	RBI/162	Runs Scored/162
1. Killebrew – 42.91	Gehrig – 153.93	Gehrig – 145.68
2. Thome – 42.45	Greenberg – 153.92	Brouthers – 142.54
3. Foxx – 40.99	Foxx – 147.54	Connor – 133.78
4. McCovey – 40.20	Anson – 135.69	Foxx – 131.42
5. Greenberg – 39.99	Mize – 135.60	Anson – 130.72
6. Gehrig – 38.03	Bottomley – 125.05	Greenberg – 126.37
7. Thomas – 37.31	Thomas – 122.01	Bagwell – 118.80
8. Mize – 36.41	Brouthers – 121.28	Terry – 116.02
9. Bagwell – 35.16	McCovey – 119.97	Mize – 113.43
10. Cepeda – 30.81	Bagwell – 119.74	Beckley – 112.06
11. Murray – 27.88	Killebrew – 118.62	Thome – 109.80
12. Perez – 25.41	Thome – 117.85	Chance – 109.40
13. Bottomley – 19.26	Terry – 111.67	Thomas – 106.97
14. Terry – 15.95	Cepeda – 110.97	Sisler – 104.60
15. Kelly – 15.80	Perez – 110.76	Bottomley – 103.51
16. Connor – 11.40	Beckley – 110.52	Killebrew – 96.08
17. Brouthers – 10.62	Connor – 109.25	McCovey – 94.82
18. Sisler – 8.31	Kelly – 108.89	Cepeda – 91.95

19. Anson – 6.34	Murray – 106.04	Murray – 90.0
20. Beckley – 6.08	Sisler – 95.97	Kelly – 87.43
21. Chance – 2.74	Chance – 81.71	Perez – 85.28

THE DEFENSIVE COMPARISONS

	dWAR/162	Assists/162	Errors/162	RF/162 to League
1.	Connor: +.520	Bagwell – 134.14	Thome – 9.77	Terry: + 102.06
2.	Chance: +.3986	Murray – 128.56	Bagwell – 10.15	Kelly: + 45.36
3.	Anson: +.320	Sisler – 127.82	Murray – 11.52	Greenberg: + 22.68
4.	Beckley: - .025	Terry – 115.85	Perez – 11.89	Anson: + 19.44
5.	Terry: - .031	Thome – 198.26	Killebrew – 12.88	Beckley: + 12.96
6.	Kelly: - .128	McCovey – 106.57	Foxx – 13.47	Murray: + 8.10
7.	Brouthers: - .169	Foxx – 106.21	Mize – 13.55	McCovey: + 3.24
8.	Foxx: - .422	Greenberg – 105.57	Thomas – 13.91	Connor: 0
9.	Perez: - .442	Mize – 1056.16	Terry – 14.43	Chance: - 3.24
10.	Greenberg: - .533	Kelly – 104.85	Kelly – 14.73	Brouthers: - 4.86
11.	Bagwell: - .564	Killebrew – 103.60	Gehrig – 14.94	Bottomley: - 9.72
12.	Sisler: - .619	Chance – 103.28	Greenberg – 15.16	Mize: - 19.44
13.	Murray: - .642	Cepeda – 101.37	Cepeda – 16.23	Thome: - 21.06
14.	Mize: - .659	Perez – 95.11	Bottomley – 19.61	Bagwell: - 27.54
15.	Gehrig: - .694	Beckley – 92.15	McCovey – 20.32	Cepeda: - 40.50
16.	Cepeda: - 1.12	Thomas – 86.44	Sisler – 22.49	Perez: - 40.50
17.	Thome: - 1.38	Gehrig – 84.16	Chance – 22.66	Foxx: - 42.12
18.	Bottomley: - 1.39	Connor – 80.83	Beckley – 33.68	Sisler: - 43.74
19.	Killebrew: - 1.400	Anson – 76.36	Anson – 51.11	Killebrew: - 46.98
20.	Thomas: - 1.61	Brouthers – 68.02	Brouthers – 54.16	Gehrig: - 68.04
21.	McCovey: - 1.66	Bottomley – 36.41	Connor – 56.21	Thomas: - 79.38

OBSERVATIONS AND COMMENTARY

Noticeable movements from JAWS to SAWS:

Dan Brouthers climbs from 6th to 2nd
Hank Greenberg goes from 12th to 6th
Frank Chance moves from 19th to 8th
Cap Anson moves from 3rd to 9th
Eddie Murray falls from 11th to 18th

Only eleven of the 21 players stay within 60% of the highest score (5.202). Frank Thomas at 5.29 is the median.

1. Lou Gehrig – 1923-1939, WAR 1st, JAWS 1st

   What needs to be said? He leads in WAR, JAWS and SAWS. And he probably will lead for eternity. The spread between Gehrig and Brouthers is .75 wins per effective season. He wraps up first in oWAR handily as well as he is first in eight of the offensive comparisons. Only his defensive numbers are mediocre as he comes in fifteenth in dWAR. On top of these statistics he had nineteen league leaderships in the six main batting categories, seven consecutive All-Star games after they began in 1933 and two MVPs as well as 2130 consecutive games played until Cal Ripken broke the record in the 1990s. The nineteen league leaderships give him a dominance ranking of thirteenth. (See last section of book entitled Position Player Consolidations) His special election is well known due to his untimely death from amyotrophic lateral sclerosis.

2. Dan Brouthers – 1879-1996, 1904, WAR 6th, JAWS 6th

   Brouthers has fewer effective seasons due to fewer games played within a season in the 1880s. He was the most dominant player of the 1800s as he pulled in 29 league leaderships in BA, OBP, SLG, OPS, HR and RBI. Those give him a fourth-place spot in dominance rankings. He even closed the gap with Gehrig in oWAR to .48 wins. His name is prominent in the higher rankings of oWAR, where he is second, and dWAR where he is seventh, so SAWS properly moves him up to second in the first baseman room. He was first in BA, third in OPB, first in SO/BB, second in OPS+ and second in runs scored. The Veterans Committee of 1936 gave him a 50.6% vote and the 1945 Old Timers Committee voted him in. He was probably the best choice of all the candidates voted in by that committee.

3. Jimmie Foxx – 1925-1945, WAR 2nd, JAWS 2nd

   The "Beast" was a power hitter to say the least and his offensive comparison rankings bear that out as he comes in third in oWAR. He was second in OPB, SLG, OPS and runs created. He was third in OPS+, season adjusted home runs and runs batted in. His .325 BA wasn't bad either. He collected three MVPs and nine All-Star appointments after they began in 1933. He had 22 league leaderships in the six main batting categories and is eighth in dominance. His defense grades out as decent in eighth place for dWAR. But "Double X", as he was also known, did not get chosen until his eighth ballot with only 79.2%. His drinking probably had something to do with that. Image can be a serious concern.

4. Johnny Mize – 1936-1953, WAR 9th, JAWS 8th

If nothing else Mize had my favorite nickname, "The Big Cat." He also had power to compare with the above three and his offensive comparisons prove that. He was fourth in oWAR as he was third in SLG, fourth in OPS and OPS+ and fifth in season adjusted RBI. He did not fare as well in dWAR slotting in at fourteenth, but his assists, errors and range factor were all above that ranking. He snatched up some fifteen league leaderships in the six main batting categories which rates him fifteenth in dominance. He also had ten All-Star games but his vote into the Hall took thirteen unsuccessful ballots and a Veterans Committee in 1981. The writers were much tougher to please than today.

5. Roger Connor – 1880-1897, WAR 4th, JAWS 4th

Roger Connor played in the shadow of Dan Brouthers and he still garnered seven league leaderships. He was the career HR champion with 138 (or 124 if you do not count homers in the Players League) until Babe Ruth came along. His offensive comparisons are slightly above median as he was sixth in oWAR with third in SO/BB ratio, seventh in OPS+ and third in runs scored. His defense shines with the top dWAR. Unbelievably, he was not considered on any ballot until his election in 1976 by a Veterans Committee. Talk about slipping through the cracks.

6. Hank Greenberg – 1930-1947, WAR 14th, JAWS 12th

If anyone deserves more recognition it is Hank Greenberg. He missed over four seasons to WWII and still put up impressive numbers. He had eight league leaderships in the main batting categories, two MVPs and four consecutive All-Star games in only nine full seasons played. He is one of only six players (not counting Barry Bonds) who have an OPS greater than 1.00. He has the eleventh best season adjusted home run rate for all position players ahead of Mays and Aaron. He was fifth in oWAR and tenth in dWAR. In the offensive comparison categories, he was second in RBI, third in SLG, OPS and runs created, fourth in OPS+, fifth in OBP and home runs, and sixth in runs scored. Yet he was not voted into the Hall until his tenth ballot with only 85%. Short career and anti-Semitism are my guesses.

7. Jeff Bagwell – 1991-2005, WAR 5th, JAWS 5th

Bagwell was an impressive first baseman. He had above average offensive capabilities across all categories and good defensive capabilities especially in assists and errors. He was Rookie of the Year and collected one MVP. He only had three league leaderships, one each in SLG, OPS an RBI so he wasn't truly dominant. So, what is the problem if he ranks seventh in SAWS and fifth in both WAR and JAWS? His eighth in oWAR and eleventh in dWAR are not bad either. The cloud of PEDs which in his case are purely circumstantial. But like I have told many a person, it is enough evidence for me. He is not getting my vote.

8. Frank Chance – 1898-1914, WAR 19th, JAWS 19th

Chance is a complete mystery to me at this level of SAWS. Every category but his SO/BB ratio is in the lower half of the offensive rankings and some are rock bottom such as SLG, runs created, season adjusted home runs and runs batted in. And his oWAR still shows eleventh. He only had one league leadership, but he did steal 403 bases. He was better in the defensive rankings as he comes in third and has one of the only three positive dWARs at first base. In my opinion, the "Peerless Leader" had more reputation from the expression "Tinker to Evers to Chance" than he did quality. He also had a lot of time as a manager. After eight writers' ballots with a maximum of 72.5% the 1946 Old Timers Committee selected him and several other dubious choices including his teammates Joe Tinker and Johnny Evers which seem to be elected as a group bootstrapping each other.

9. Cap Anson – 1871-1897, WAR 3rd, JAWS 3rd

Cap Anson is generally considered the first superstar collecting 3000 hits, easily if you count his games in the National Association from 1871-1875. He had upper level presence in the comparative categories and eighteen league leaderships giving him a dominance ranking of sixteenth. He was second in SO/BB, fourth in runs batted in, and fifth in runs scored and batting average. His was seventh in oWAR and third in dWAR with a positive number. Many of his seasons came nowhere near having 154 or 162 games so the game of "what if" looms large with Anson. The 1936 Veterans Committee recognized him with 50.6% of the vote and the 1939 Old Timers Committee plucked him out of the crowd. Today, however, he would be shunned as he was an inveterate racist. Still a Hall of Famer from the statistics.

10. Bill Terry – 1923-1936, WAR 15th, JAWS 15th

A contact hitter with a high BA which was second in the room but little else. He hit .401 once but the league also hit over .300 that year. He has a weak oWAR of fourteenth to say the least. He had a much better dWAR of fifth with a first place in range factor and a fourth spot in assists. He did make three All-Star teams late in his career. He was selected on his fifteenth ballot with only 77.2%. Again, it is difficult to justify some of these players the closer you sink to or below the median. Close but no cigar here. He also became a cohort of Frankie Frisch on the Veterans Committees of 1967-73.

11. Frank Thomas – 1990-2008, WAR 7th, JAWS 8th

The median player has good numbers. A .301 BA with 521 HRs. He is slightly above the median otherwise, but this is a tough room offensively. His oWAR comes in at ninth. He had ten league leaderships but no dominance ranking and four more league leaderships in BB. He pulled in two MVPs and was considered nine additional times. His defense was weak as his dWAR is twentieth and a clear indication of why he was a DH. The key to his discussion is that he was a DH for 1310 games. He still pulled down 83.7% of the vote on the first ballot. Not in my Hall of Fame, Frank.

12. Jim Thome – 1991-2012, WAR 8th, JAWS 9th

I find it odd that the two DHs at first base are back to back. I can talk about Thome's offensive and defensive rankings but the key to this conversation is 612 home runs with 813 DH games involved. Excluding Barry Bonds, he is ranked eighth in career homers. Not in my Hall, Jim, even if you did get 89.8% on the first ballot. In fact, I cannot see letting these two in as I think it would be an insult to players like Lou Gehrig. Gehrig played every day, and I mean during the day in the hot sun, showered in non-airconditioned clubhouses and rode on trains overnight to get to the next city. These two sat on the bench and rested their legs for over 2121 games, just nine short of what Gehrig played consecutively.

13. Willie McCovey – 1959-1980, WAR 11th, JAWS 10th

Willie's offensive comparison rankings float around the median and put him tenth in oWAR but his dWAR comes in dead last. Offensively he was fourth in season adjusted home runs but next to last in BA. But I am sure that the rankings would not have affected his first ballot vote of 81.4%. He hit 521 homers, collected the Rookie of the Year Award, one MVP and twelve league leaderships with his six All-Star games. But he also had 573 games as DH. Another one missing my vote.

14. Harmon Killebrew – 1954-1975, WAR, 13th, JAWS 14th

If anyone is in the Hall for hitting home runs it has to be Killebrew although it took four ballots for him to reach 83.1%. He possesses the second lowest BA for a position player at .256. He is third in season adjusted home runs behind Ruth and Kiner. He only reached thirteenth in oWAR. He did pick up eleven All-Star appointments, one MVP and eleven league leaderships of which six are for home runs. He was a terrible fielder, being nineteenth at dWAR, at third, left field and first base and did get 145 games in at DH. I feel like some of the writers. He won't get my vote ever.

15. George Sisler – 1915-1930, WAR 16th, JAWS 13th

A hitter with a high average and limited power. He batted .400 twice during the early "live ball" era. He won one MVP (the AL did not allow repeat MVPs in the 1920s) and actually had another 2.3 WAR from pitching. He held the season record for hits at 257 for 84 years. He had a 41-game hitting streak. Despite all this he was below median offensively in category comparisons with a fifteenth slot in oWAR and generally weak in defense with a twelfth position. He tied for third with Gehrig in BA and came in seventh in SO/BB ratio. His worst categories were eighteenth in home runs and twentieth in runs batted in. He was elected on his fourth ballot with 85.8%. Not a bad player. Just nothing great or famous jumping out at me.

16. Jake Beckley – 1888-1907, WAR 12th, JAWS 16th

All I ever remember about Beckley is that he held the record for games played at first base until Eddie Murray broke it. His offensive comparative categories do him no good at all as he stays at level sixteen in oWAR. He climbed to a hair above median with a tenth slot in BA and runs scored and an eleventh spot in batting average. But dWAR is impressive at fourth place. But defense is not what one looks for at first base. He did amass .4% to 1.2% in two ballots in 1936 and 1942 and was resurrected into immortal fame by the 1971 Veterans Committee. What a crock!

17. Orlando Cepeda – 1958-1974, WAR 18th, JAWS 18th

The "Baby Bull" stayed on the ballot sheet for fifteen tries and inched up to 73.5% of the votes so the writers were not completely sure of him. The Veterans Committee of 1999 did anoint him with fame. Except for his home run statistic his comparative statistics are all bottom half numbers. He was next to last in SO/BB ratio. Seventeenth in oWAR and sixteenth in dWAR are not impressive. He did lead the league in homers once and runs batted in twice. He pocketed one MVP, the Rookie of the Year Award and seven All-Star appointments. He played in three World Series and batted all of .171. A very good player but the Hall of Fame is for great and famous players.

18. Eddie Murray – 1977-1997, WAR 10th, JAWS 11th

Murray played in a lot of games and his quantity was not necessarily offset by his quality. Other than home runs he does not crack the median on the way up in any offensive comparison category. Consequently, he is very low in oWAR at nineteenth. In 21 years he had eight All-Star appointments, one league leadership in OBP, and three Gold Gloves. He did round up the Rookie of the Year award. He had 573 games as DH but was not as bad of a fielder coming in at thirteenth in dWAR. His 504 home runs must have gone a long way with the writers because he collected 85.3% of the vote on the first ballot. A little non-descript for me. SAWS may have taken him down eight notches but averaging in his best seven years for JAWS took him down one notch and indicated his overall direction.

19. Tony Perez – 1964-1986, WAR 17th, JAWS 17th

I congratulate Tony for playing 23 years. Very few get there. But years are pure quantity. He is not only very low in season adjusted numbers, but he is low in traditional numbers. He is next to last in oWAR but he is ninth in dWAR. He is last in runs scored, OPB and SO/BB ratio and next to last in OPS+. He came in on his ninth ballot with 77.2%. Some of his attraction had to be the coattails of Joe Morgan and Johnny Bench and the "Big Red Machine." He just does not have the numbers.

20. Jim Bottomley – 1922-1937, WAR 20th, JAWS 20th

Bottomley has some semi-respectable comparative numbers offensively but not good numbers defensively. He was sixth in runs batted in and tenth in BA. Yet he still checks in at eighteenth in both oWAR and dWAR. He did win one MVP and three league leaderships but that is about all you can say about this guy. On twelve writer's ballots he collected 33% but the 1974 Veterans Committee picked him out of a crowd. Maybe he had a familiar face. He just blends in with a lot of other faces to me.

21. High Pockets Kelly – 1915-1932, WAR 21st, JAWS 21st

This one is just wrong. Kelly did have a league leadership in HR once and RBI twice and he wasn't a bad fielder. You can look above to see the poor comparative statistics but note that he was next to last in OPB, runs created and runs scored while he was last in OPS and oWAR. His oWAR is about one-fourth of Gehrig's. He worked his way up to 1.9% of the vote on seven ballots before the 1973 Veterans Committee adorned him with fame. An embarrassment to the Hall.

THE OTHERS

Todd Helton comes up in 2019 sporting a 4.7796 SAWS, a 61.2 WAR and a 53.9 JAWS. That would put him 14th, 13th and tied for 11th respectively, in the current room of 21. It is not exactly impressive to be below both the 60% cutoff and the median. He has no particular awards or league leaderships to rely on either. Top that with the thin air of Denver, Colorado and you dampen his traditional power stats. Don't expect my vote even if I had one.

Steve Garvey was popular but has a 2.88 SAWS. End of conversation.

I must continue to ignore the plaintive wail of the Gil Hodges fan club. His SAWS of 3.57, WAR of 41.8 and JAWS of 39.6 put him third from the last in the room. But he was loved and obviously a great ambassador for the game.

Keith Hernandez comes much closer to deserving election with a 5.09 SAWS and his eleven Gold Gloves with an MVP would do the trick for me. Defense, though, is not how first basemen get enshrined. Cocaine use doesn't help your image, either.

Although Albert Pujols will probably waltz in once he retires he would not get my vote on the first ballot because the second half of his career is too poor compared to the first half and he has become a designated hitter. His current SAWS is about 6.49 and will probably dwindle over the next few years reflecting his true overall worth.

THIRD BASEMEN

THE SEASONS

	Actual	Total Effective	Effective Seasons at 3B
1.	Brooks Robinson – 23	17.2037	17.1712
2.	George Brett – 21	16.0466	10.0016
3.	Paul Molitor – 21	16.1623	4.7311
4.	Deacon White – 20	9.3875	4.9225
5.	Chipper Jones – 19	14.3128	11.7323
6.	Mike Schmidt – 18	13.9408	12.9959
7.	Wade Boggs – 18	14.0126	12.9776
8.	Eddie Mathews – 17	13.912	13.04
9.	Pie Traynor – 17	11.5521	11.2874
10.	George Kell – 15	10.3251	9.9099
11.	Ron Santo – 15	13.3964	12.8793
12.	Jimmy Collins – 14	10.4198	10.2126
13.	Frank Baker – 13	9.5178	6.5982
14.	Freddie Lindstrom – 13	8.2428	4.8608

THE RANKINGS

	SAWS	WAR	JAWS
1.	Mike Schmidt – 7.67	Schmidt – 106.8	Schmidt – 82.8
2.	Eddie Mathews – 6.94	Mathews – 96.6	Mathews – 75.6
3.	"Home Run" Baker – 6.60	Boggs – 91.4	Boggs – 73.9
4.	Wade Boggs – 6.52	Brett – 88.7	Brett – 71
5.	Chipper Jones – 5.95	Jones – 85.2	Jones – 66.0
6.	George Brett – 5.51	Robinson – 78.4	Santo – 62.2
7.	Ron Santo – 5.27	Molitor – 75.7	Robinson – 62.1
8.	Jimmy Collins – 5.12	Santo – 70.5	Molitor – 57.7
9.	Deacon White – 4.87	Baker – 62.8	Baker – 54.8
10.	Paul Molitor – 4.68	Collins – 53.3	Collins – 45.9
11.	Brooks Robinson – 4.56	White – 45.7	White – 35.9
12.	George Kell – 3.62	Kell – 37.4	Kell – 32.6
13.	Freddie Lindstrom – 3.45	Traynor – 36.3	Traynor – 31.0
14.	Pie Traynor – 3.14	Lindstrom – 28.4	Lindstrom – 27.3

THE OFFENSIVE COMPARISONS

	BA	OBP	SLG	OPS
1.	Boggs - .328	Boggs - .415	Jones - .529	Jones - .930
2.	Traynor - .320	Jones - .401	Schmidt - .527	Schmidt - .908
3.	White - .312	Schmidt - .380	Mathews - .509	Mathews - .885
4.	Lindstrom - .311	Mathews - .376	Brett - .487	Boggs - .858
5.	Baker - .307	Brett - .3693	Santo - .464	Brett - .857
6.	Kell - .3065	Molitor - .3691	Lindstrom - .449	Santo - .826
7.	Molitor – .3063	Kell - .367	Kell - .448	Kell - .817
8.	Brett - .305	Baker - .363	Boggs - .443	Baker - .805
9.	Jones - .303	Santo - .3624	Baker - .442	Lindstrom - .800
10.	Collins - .294	Traynor - .3621	Traynor - .435	Traynor - .797
11.	Santo - .277	Lindstrom - .351	Molitor - .414	Molitor - .791
12.	Mathews - .271	White - .346	Collins - .409	Collins - .752
13.	Schmidt - .2675	Collins - .343	Robinson - .401	White - .740
14.	Robinson - .2673	Robinson - .322	White - .393	Robinson - .723

	oWAR/162	Runs Created/162	SO/BB Ratio	OPS+
1.	Mathews – 6.77	Jones – 137.29	Kell - .4622	Schmidt - 147
2.	Schmidt – 6.58	Schmidt – 126.03	Boggs - .5276	Mathews - 143
3.	Baker – 6.24	Boggs – 124.89	Traynor - .5890	Jones - 141
4.	Jones – 6.17	Mathews – 123.35	Collins - .6244	Brett - 135
5.	Boggs – 5.81	Brett – 117.34	White - .7175	Baker - 135
6.	Brett – 5.28	Molitor – 115.89	Baker - .7315	Boggs - 131
7.	White – 5.24	Lindstrom – 107.85	Brett - .8285	White - 127
8.	Santo – 4.97	Santo – 102.94	Lindstrom - .8263	Santo - 125
9.	Molitor – 4.68	Traynor – 102.84	Jones - .9319	Molitor - 122
10.	Collins – 4.09	Kell – 98.98	Mathews – 1.0298	Collins - 113
11.	Traynor – 3.47	Baker – 98.97	Molitor – 1.1371	Kell - 112
12.	Kell – 3.43	White – 95.97	Robinson – 1.1512	Lindstrom 110
13.	Lindstrom – 3.25	Collins – 90.5	Santo – 1.2121	Traynor - 107
14.	Robinson – 2.78	Robinson – 78.76	Schmidt – 1.2495	Robinson - 104

	HR/162	RBI/162	Runs Scored/162
1.	Schmidt – 39.31	Schmidt – 114.41	White – 121.44
2.	Mathews – 36.80	Jones – 113.39	Jones – 113.12
3.	Jones – 32.70	Traynor – 110.2	Molitor – 110.26
4.	Santo – 25.53	White – 105.25	Lindstrom – 108.58

5. Brett – 19.75	Mathews – 104.44	Mathews – 108.47
6. Robinson – 15.58	Baker – 104.12	Schmidt – 108.03
7. Molitor – 14.48	Brett – 99.46	Boggs – 107.97
8. Lindstrom – 12.50	Santo – 99.36	Traynor – 102.41
9. Baker – 10.09	Lindstrom – 94.51	Collins – 101.25
10. Boggs – 8.42	Collins – 94.34	Brett – 98.65
11. Kell – 7.55	Kell – 84.26	Baker – 93.19
12. Collins – 6.24	Molitor – 80.89	Kell – 85.23
13. White – 2.55	Robinson – 78.88	Santo – 84.95
14. Traynor - .433	Boggs – 72.36	Robinson – 71.61

THE DEFENSIVE COMPARISONS

dWAR/162	Assists/162	Errors/162
1. Robinson: + 2. 27	Baker – 478.2	Robinson – 15.32
2. Collins: + 1.61	Schmidt – 388.2	Kell – 16.75
3. Schmidt: + 1.31	Brett – 369.3	Boggs – 17.45
4. Baker: + 1.02	Collins – 362.5	Jones – 19.01
5. Boggs: + .992	Robinson – 361.4	Mathews – 22.47
6. Santo: + .649	Santo – 355.7	Schmidt – 24.08
7. Mathews: + .402	Molitor – 346.4	Santo – 24.61
8. Lindstrom: + .315	Kell – 333.3	Molitor – 24.89
9. Traynor: + .182	Mathews – 331.4	Brett – 26.10
10. White: + .1704	White – 328.9	Lindstrom – 27.77
11. Kell: + .155	Boggs – 327.2	Traynor – 28.70
12. Brett: + .137	Lindstrom – 316	Collins – 45.53
13. Jones: - .069	Traynor – 311.9	Baker – 48.8
14. Molitor: -.4269	Jones – 293.8	White – 90.20

Double Plays/162	FP/162 to League	RF/162 to League
1. Baker – 39.40	Robinson - .971/.953	Schmidt: + 45.36
2. Molitor – 39.10	Kell - .969/.954	Santo: + 34.02
3. Robinson – 35.91	Boggs - .962/.951	Collins: + 30.78
4. Schmidt – 34.63	Lindstrom - .959/.948	Traynor: + 30.78
5. Boggs – 32.59	Mathews - .956/.950	Robinson: + 17.82
6. Kell – 30.88	Schmidt - .955/.949	Molitor: + 16.20
7. Santo – 30.67	Santo - .954/.948	Baker: + 11.34
8. Brett – 30.65	Jones - .954/.953	Lindstrom: + 4.86
9. Mathews – 28.30	Brett - .951/.953	Mathews: + 1.62

10. Lindstrom – 27.78	Molitor - .950/.952	Boggs: + 1.62
11. Traynor – 26.85	Traynor - .947/.947	Brett: 0
12. White – 23.97	Baker - .943/.937	Kell: - 3.24
13. Jones – 23.52	Collins .929/.907	White: -29.61
14. Collins – 22.03	White - .853/.861	Jones: - 37.26

OBSERVATIONS AND COMMENTARY

Noticeable movements from JAWS to SAWS:

Brooks Robinson moves from a tie for 6th to 11th
Frank "Home Run" Baker moves from 9th to 3rd

Nine of the fourteen make the 60% cutoff (4.60). The median is 5.19.

1. Mike Schmidt – 1972-1989, WAR 1st, JAWS 1st

Schmidt is already ranked overall as the twelfth greatest player in addition to being first at third base in WAR, JAWS and SAWS. I can only imagine what his rank would be if he had a BA of .300 or better. 548 home runs, twelve All-Star selections, nine Gold Gloves, three MVPs, a World Series MVP and 25 league leaderships which makes him seventh in dominance. Top that off with the above comparative statistics in both offense and defense that climb to the top or near top. His oWAR is second and his dWAR is third making him a very complete player. A first ballot Hall of Famer with 96.5% of the vote.

2. Eddie Mathews – 1952-1968, WAR 2nd, JAWS 2nd

The only Brave who played in Boston, Milwaukee and Atlanta. He hit 512 homers and gave Schmidt a run for his money in the offensive comparisons. He was second in OPS+ and season adjusted homers, third in SLG and OPS and fourth in OPB. He even beat Schmidt in season adjusted oWAR and came in first. He only had three league leaderships, though, so he was not dominant. Defensively he was middle of the road with a seven slot in dWAR. His awards were limited to nine All-Star selections. He did appear in three World Series but had a BA of only.200. It was the fifth ballot before he collected 79.4% of the vote. Should have been sooner.

3. Frank "Home Run" Baker – 1908-1922, WAR 9th, JAWS 9th

The nickname was acquired by hitting two home runs in a World Series but he hit ten season adjusted homers which is quite a bit for his era. He also led the league in homers four times. He appeared in six World Series and batted a strong .363. His comparative statistics bounce around from above to below median, but he is third in oWAR and fourth in dWAR. Offensively he was fifth in OPS and BA. Defensively he was first in assists and double plays. Twelve ballots came and went with a maximum vote of about 30% before the Veterans Committee of 1955 put him in the Hall. Going from ninth in JAWS to third in SAWS with such a short career still leaves him suspect.

4. Wade Boggs – 1982-1999, WAR 3rd, JAWS 3rd

A .328 BA cannot be ignored even though he had limited power but still fifth in oWAR. He was first in BA and OBP, second in SO/BB, third in runs created and fourth in OPS. He was fifth in dWAR by being third in errors and fielding percentage. He saw twelve All-Star appointments, eight Silver Sluggers and two Gold Gloves added to his portfolio. He had thirteen league leaderships, including five in BA and six in OPB, in the main batting categories as well. He batted .286 in two World Series. A first ballot success with 91.9%.

5. Chipper Jones – 1993-2012, WAR 5th, JAWS 5th

Amazing offensive statistics, traditional or season adjusted, elevate Jones to a high plane but only fourth in oWAR. He was first in SLG, OPS and runs created. He was second in OBP, runs batted in and runs scored. He was third in OPS+ and season adjusted homers. Awards are plentiful as well. Three league leaderships, one each in BA, OBP and OPS. Slash stats above .300/.400/.500. 468 home runs. One MVP, two Silver Sluggers, eight All-Star squads, second in Rookie of the Year balloting and three World Series with one home run and six runs batted in. What's the catch? He is the first true third basemen, other than Molitor who was more of a DH, to be selected for the Hall with a negative dWAR which was next to last in the room. That logically comes from being last in assists and range factor and next to last in double plays. First ballot winner with 97.2%. I would have been part of the 2.8% based on his defense.

6. George Brett – 1973-1993, WAR 3rd, JAWS 3rd

Brett is slightly above the median and a little more middle of the road offensively (oWAR of sixth) than I perceived him to be which makes his 98.2% first ballot a little overstated. He was fifth in OPB, OPS, OPS+, and season adjusted runs created and home runs. He is still quite deserving of the Hall as he racked up one MVP, one Gold Glove, thirteen All-Star appointments, three Silver Sluggers, nine league leaderships, a 30-game hitting streak, two World Series with a .373 BA and 3154 hits. The last entry can be questioned in connection with slightly over 500 games as DH. His defense was definitely middle of the road for a Hall of Famer as he was two points below league average in fielding percentage and exactly equal to league range factor at third base. He did have tremendous name recognition and image...some of it thanks to a "pine tar" home run. I would have been part of the 1.8% again. Just not a first ballot vote from me.

7. Ron Santo – 1960-1974, WAR 8th, JAWS 6th

Santo's comparisons try to compete favorably with the upper six players offensively but comes in eighth in oWAR and compares better defensively with fifth place. He had some hidden power in that he was fourth in seasonal home runs and SLG. He won five Gold Gloves and was selected to nine All-Star teams. Santo, with fifteen actual seasons, played almost as many effective seasons as both Schmidt who had seventeen actual seasons and Mathews who had eighteen actual seasons. He had almost six more season adjusted home runs than Brett and ten more than Robinson. He was second only to Schmidt in seasonal range factor above league and twice as good as Robinson. He had .1 season adjusted RBI less than Brett. And he did it all as a closet diabetic. Santo suffered through fifteen ballots before being elected posthumously by the Veterans Committee of 2012. It should have come much sooner.

8. Jimmy Collins – 1895-1908, WAR 10th, JAWS 10th

Collins was definitely low in the offensive comparisons (tenth in oWAR) but strong in dWAR (second) and range factor above league. He did lead the league in home runs once and total bases once. His fielding percentage to league was .921 to .907. But, he was next to last in runs created and OPB and third from the bottom in SLG, OPS and home runs. Through seven ballots he scratched out about 32% before the 1945 Old Timers Committee brought him in. He was the first third baseman chosen. He is a good solid player but not great or famous.

9. Deacon White – 1871-1890, WAR 11th, JAWS 11th

Along with Cap Anson he is one of the first players in the original National Association. True to the era his was proficient in runs scored and runs batted in. He led the league in BA twice and RBI three times. He also led the league in SLG and OPS once each. He had a good BA of .312 which kept his oWAR at seventh. His fielding was weak though, but then again, fielding was not good at all in the early days. He was extremely versatile as he played all nine positions. He received 1.3% from the 1936 Veterans Committee and then lay dormant until the 2013 Veterans Committee honored him. This is a tough call, but the original players of the National Association deserve to be represented.

10. Paul Molitor – 1978-1998, WAR 7th, JAWS 8th

Unable to find a fit anywhere as a defensive player he became a DH for 1174 games and 1495 games were scattered around the field but 791 were at third base. Offensively he had a good BA with moderate power but only came in ninth in oWAR. He is scattered all around the comparison rankings as well. Since his defense was lacking and his body was injury prone, DH was all that was left. A .306 BA and 3319 hits pretty much assured him a plaque in Cooperstown. His first ballot numbers rose to 85.2%. I would not have voted for him or any other player who was primarily a DH.

11. Brooks Robinson – 1955-1977, WAR 6th, JAWS 7th

I am sure some are surprised by Robinson falling to eleventh out of fifteen but to be honest with you he has terrible offensive rankings, including last in oWAR, which is what most Hall of Famers rely on for their ranking. He was actually last in seven offensive categories. His defense was otherworldly – and clearly first in the room – and that supersedes any offensive lacks and marks him as one of the greatest. He won sixteen Gold Gloves, was elected to fifteen All-Star squads, and won one regular season MVP and one World Series MVP. He collected 92% of the writers' votes on the first ballot. Despite his low SAWS ranking he stays in.

12. George Kell – 1943-1957, WAR 12th, JAWS 12th

He did get elected to ten All-Star squads and led the league in BA one year as he did have a good eye at the plate. His offensive statistics are middle of the pack to down and his defensive statistics are erratic. His best categories are first in SO/BB ratio and second in fielding percentage. Twelfth in oWAR and eleventh in dWAR are nothing special. After fifteen ballots with a maximum of 36.8% of the votes the Veterans Committee of 1983 brought him on board. He seemed like a very good player, but I believe the Hall calls for more than just very good.

13. Freddie Lindstrom – 1924-1936, WAR 14th, JAWS 14th

Lindstrom may be more infamous than famous for a couple of popcorn hop ground balls in the 1924 World Series. His comparison statistics are median to low for both offense and defense. dWAR at eighth was much better than oWAR at thirteenth. He is so mixed in with the middle he is almost invisible. He rounded up all of 4.4% of the votes in five ballots and once again a committee, this time in 1976, comes to his aid. I have no explanation.

14. Pie Traynor – 1920-1937, WAR 13th, JAWS 13th

A decent BA of .320 and two All-Star appointments late in his career are all I can find to brag about. Except for his season adjusted RBI and his season adjusted range factor to league number I think all of his comparison statistics are in the lower half of all rankings. His oWAR was ninth and dWAR was eleventh. He somehow found 76.5% of the votes after seven ballots. He wasn't all that bad…he just wasn't all that good. Another inexplicable situation.

THE OTHERS

Edgar Martinez is pretty much in the middle of the pack when it comes to SAWS, WAR and JAWS. (5.71/68.4/56.0) His slash stats are much more impressive at .312/.418/.515 with an OPS of .933 and an adjusted OPS of 147. The writers aren't all that impressed, but he has acquired 70.4% of the vote on his ninth ballot in 2018. A DH won't get my vote.

Scott Rolen has good numbers as well with a SAWS of 5.85, WAR of 70.2 and JAWS of 56.9 but not nearly the offensive punch of Martinez. He has a great dWAR of 20.6 and a Rookie of the Year award but only 10.2% support from the writers. He deserves more respect but does not possess a lot of *fame* though.

Dick "don't all me Richie" Allen had similar numbers with a 5.875 SAWS, 58.7 WAR and a 52.3 JAWs as well as Rookie of the Year, one MVP and a powerful OPS+ of 156. His defense was terrible with a negative 16.3 dWAR and his attitude may have even been worse. From fourteen ballots he climbed to an 18.9%. More infamy than fame but that dWAR sews it up for me.

SECOND BASEMEN

SEASONS

	Actual	Total Effective	Effective at 2B
1.	Eddie Collins – 25	16.4005	16.1488
2.	Rogers Hornsby – 23	12.9781	9.3567
3.	Joe Morgan – 22	14.9033	14.7757
4.	Nap Lajoie – 21	14.8230	12.3676
5.	Craig Biggio – 20	16.329	11.7659
6.	Charlie Gehringer – 19	13.3519	13.2723
7.	Rod Carew – 19	13.3596	6.4904
8.	Frankie Frisch – 19	13.5837	10.5487
9.	Nellie Fox – 19	13.9026	13.8663
10.	Red Schoendienst – 19	11.995	10.7917
11.	Johnny Evers – 18	10.5816	10.3532
12.	Bid McPhee – 18	12.8745	12.8491
13.	Roberto Alomar – 17	13.8025	13.6324
14.	Bill Mazeroski – 17	12.5764	12.5764
15.	Ryne Sandberg – 16	12.6413	11.8187
16.	Billy Herman – 15	11.5960	11.0069
17.	Bobby Doerr – 14	11.1765	11.1765
18.	Tony Lazzeri – 14	10.1749	8.7298
19.	Joe Gordon – 11	9.3523	9.1856
20.	Jackie Robinson – 10	7.7699	4.3871

THE RANKINGS

	SAWS	WAR	JAWS
1.	Rogers Hornsby – 9.79	Hornsby – 127	Hornsby – 100.3
2.	Jackie Robinson – 7.90	Collins – 124	Collins – 94.1
3.	Eddie Collins – 7.56	Lajoie – 107.4	Lajoie – 83.9
4.	Napoleon Lajoie – 7.25	Morgan – 100.6	Morgan – 79.9
5.	Joe Morgan – 6.75	Carew – 81.3	Gehringer – 65.6
6.	Joe Gordon – 6.11	Gehringer – 80.6	Carew – 65.5
7.	Charlie Gehringer – 6.04	Frisch – 70.4	Sandberg – 57.5
8.	Rod Carew – 5.98	Sandberg – 68.0	Frisch – 57.4
9.	Ryne Sandberg – 5.38	Alomar – 67.1	Robinson – 56.7
10.	Frankie Frisch – 5.18	Biggio – 65.5	Alomar – 55
11.	Tony Lazzeri – 4.91	Robinson – 61.4	Biggio – 53.7
12.	Roberto Alomar – 4.86	Gordon – 57.2	Gordon – 51.5

13. Billy Herman – 4.73	Herman – 54.8	Herman – 45.1
14. Bobby Doerr – 4.58	McPhee – 52.6	Doerr – 43.8
15. Johnny Evers – 4.51	Doerr – 51.2	Fox – 42.9
16. Bid McPhee – 4.09	Lazzeri – 50.0	Lazzeri – 42.6
17. Craig Biggio – 4.01	Fox – 49.0	McPhee – 41.0
18. Red Schoendienst – 3.23	Evers – 47.7	Evers – 40.5
19. Nellie Fox – 3.52	Schoendienst – 42.3	Schoendienst – 37.0
20. Bill Mazeroski – 2.90	Mazeroski – 36.5	Mazeroski – 31.2

THE OFFENSIVE COMPARISONS

	BA	OBP	SLG	OPS
1.	Hornsby - .358	Hornsby - .434	Hornsby - .577	Hornsby – 1.01
2.	Lajoie - .338	Collins - .424	Gehringer - .480	Gehringer - .884
3.	Collins - .333	Robinson - .409	Robinson - .474	Robinson - .883
4.	Carew - .328	Gehringer - .404	Lazzeri - .467	Collins - .853
5.	Gehringer - .320	Carew - .393	Lajoie - .4664	Lajoie - .847
6.	Frisch - .316	Morgan - .392	Gordon - .4656	Lazzeri - .846
7.	Robinson - .311	Lajoie - .3802	Doerr - .461	Doerr - .823
8.	Herman - .304	Lazzeri - .3799	Sandberg - .452	Gordon - .8225
9.	Alomar - .300	Alomar - .371	Alomar - .443	Carew - .8222
10.	Lazzeri - .292	Frisch - .369	Biggio - .433	Morgan - .819
11.	Schoendienst - .299	Herman - .367	Frisch - .432	Alomar - .814
12.	Fox - .2285	Biggio - .363	Carew - .4292	Frisch - .801
13.	Doerr - .2879	Doerr - .362	Collins - .4290	Biggio - .796
14.	Sandberg - .285	Gordon - .357	Morgan - .427	Sandberg - .795
15.	Biggio - .281	Evers - .356	Herman - .407	Herman - .774
16.	McPhee - .272	McPhee - .355	Schoendienst - .387	McPhee - .728
17.	Morgan - .271	Fox - .348	McPhee - .373	Schoendienst - .724
18.	Evers - .270	Sandberg - .344	Mazeroski - .367	Fox - .710
19.	Gordon - .268	Schoendienst - .337	Fox - .363	Evers - .690
20.	Mazeroski - .260	Mazeroski - .299	Evers - .334	Mazeroski - .667

	oWAR/162	Runs Created/162	SO/BB Ratio	Steals/162
1.	Hornsby – 9.38	Hornsby – 157.57	Fox - .3004	Morgan – 46.23
2.	Collins – 7.31	Gehringer – 128.45	Collins - .3122	Collins – 45.18
3.	Morgan – 7.01	Robinson – 122.43	Gehringer - .3137	McPhee – 44.12
4.	Robinson – 6.98	Morgan – 121.05	McPhee - .3228	Alomar – 34.34
5.	Lajoie – 6.63	Carew – 119.39	Frisch - .3736	Frisch – 30.85

6.	Carew – 6.06	Alomar – 114.11	Evers - .3766	Evers – 30.62
7.	Gehringer – 5.82	Lajoie – 113.34	Robinson - .3932	Sandberg – 27.21
8.	Alomar – 5.13	Biggio – 112.19	Schoendienst - .5710	Carew – 25.97
9.	Lazzeri – 4.86	Collins – 110.39	Herman - .5807	Lajoie – 25.64
10.	Sandberg – 4.78	Lazzeri – 109.19	Hornsby - .6541	Robinson – 25.36
11.	Biggio – 4.67	Frisch – 107.47	Lajoie - .6725	Biggio – 25.35
12.	Gordon – 4.43	Sandberg – 106.16	Doerr - .7515	Fox – 15.54
13.	Herman – 4.27	Doerr – 104.59	Gordon - .9249	Lazzeri – 14.55
14.	Frisch – 4.20	Gordon – 100.8	Lazzeri - .9942	Gehringer – 13.56
15.	Doerr – 4.14	Herman – 99.26	Carew – 1.0098	Hornsby – 10.40
16.	Evers – 3.15	Schoendienst–95.21	Alomar – 1.1047	Gordon – 9.51
17.	McPhee – 3.13	Fox – 84.52	Biggio – 1.5122	Schoendienst – 7.42
18.	Schoendienst–2.99	McPhee – 84.35	Morgan – 1.5442	Herman – 5.78
19.	Fox – 2.65	Evers – 68.23	Mazeroski – 1.5794	Doerr – 4.83
20.	Mazeroski – 1.55	Mazeroski – 65.36	Sandberg – 1.6557	Mazeroski – 2.15

	HR/162	RBI/162	Runs/162
1.	Gordon – 27.0	Hornsby – 122.06	Gehringer – 132.87
2.	Hornsby – 23.19	Lazzeri – 117.35	McPhee – 130.80
3.	Sandberg – 22.31	Doerr – 111.57	Robinson – 121.91
4.	Doerr – 19.95	Lajoie – 107.87	Hornsby – 121.67
5.	Morgan – 17.98	Gehringer – 106.88	Frisch – 112.78
6.	Biggio – 17.82	Gordon – 104.25	Collins – 111.03
7.	Robinson – 17.64	Robinson – 94.49	Morgan – 110.71
8.	Lazzeri – 17.49	Frisch – 91.58	Biggio – 110.48
9.	Alomar – 15.21	Sandberg – 83.93	Alomar – 109.26
10.	Gehringer – 13.78	McPhee – 83.27	Carew – 106.59
11.	Mazeroski – 10.97	Alomar – 82.16	Sandberg – 104.26
12.	Frisch – 7.73	Collins – 79.27	Schoendienst – 101.96
13.	Schoendienst – 7.0	Morgan – 76.02	Lajoie – 101.46
14.	Carew – 6.89	Carew – 75.98	Herman – 100.29
15.	Lajoie – 5.53	Herman – 72.35	Gordon – 97.93
16.	McPhee – 4.12	Biggio – 71.96	Doerr – 97.88
17.	Herman – 4.05	Schoendienst – 64.44	Lazerri – 96.91
18.	Collins – 2.87	Mazeroski – 61.83	Fox – 92.0
19.	Fox – 2.52	Fox – 56.82	Evers – 86.85
20.	Evers – 1.13	Evers – 50.65	Mazeroski – 61.15

THE DEFENSIVE COMPARISONS

	dWAR/162	Assists/162	Errors/162
1.	Gordon – 2.40	Hornsby – 552.18	Sandberg – 9.22
2.	Mazeroski – 1.91	Frisch – 571.26	Biggio – 13.26
3.	Frisch – 1.59	McPhee – 538.48	Alomar – 13.28
4.	Fox – 1.51	Sandberg – 538.38	Fox – 15.07
5.	Evers – 1.46	Gehringer – 532.54	Robinson – 15.50
6.	Robinson – 1.30	Mazeroski – 531.55	Schoendienst – 15.75
7.	Schoendienst – 1.27	Herman – 516.13	Mazeroski – 16.22
8.	McPhee – 1.26	Gordon – 512.32	Morgan – 16.51
9.	Doerr – 1.20	Doerr – 510.89	Doerr – 19.15
10.	Hornsby – 1.071	Lazerri – 509.16	Gehringer – 23.28
11.	Herman – 1.069	Lajoie – 506.73	Carew – 23.73
12.	Sandberg – 1.068	Evers – 494.92	Frisch – 26.54
13.	Gehringer - .801	Schoendienst – 485.84	Collins – 26.94
14.	Lajoie - .684	Alomar – 478.57	Gordon – 28.31
15.	Lazerri - .511	Morgan – 471.52	Lazzeri – 30.13
16.	Collins - .50	Robinson – 468.87	Herman – 32.16
17.	Morgan - .25	Biggio – 463.03	Hornsby – 32.81
18.	Alomar - .239	Collins – 455.76	Lajoie – 36.47
19.	Carew - .1278	Carew – 455.75	Evers – 40.86
20.	Biggio - .178	Fox – 439.19	McPhee – 61.22

	Double Plays/162	FP/162 to League	RF/162 to League
1.	Robinson – 138.36	Sandberg - .989/.981	Lajoie: + 92.34
2.	Mazeroski – 135.65	Alomar - .984/.981	McPhee: + 81
3.	Doerr – 134.84	Biggio - .984/.983	Mazeroski: + 43.74
4.	Schoendienst – 126.76	Fox - .984/.977	Doerr: + 40.50
5.	Gordon – 126.28	Robinson - .983/.975	Frisch: + 27.54
6.	Fox – 116.76	Schoendienst - .983/.975	Schoendienst: + 21.06
7.	Gehringer – 108.80	Mazeroski - .983/.976	Biggio: + 17.82
8.	Herman – 106.93	Morgan - .981/.977	Sandberg: + 16.20
9.	Alomar – 103.21	Doerr - .980/.971	Herman: + 16.20
10.	Carew – 102.25	Gehringer - .976/.968	Collins: +8.1
11.	Morgan – 101.86	Frisch - .974/.962	Evers: + 6.48
12.	Frisch – 100.68	Carew - .973/.977	Fox: + 3.24
13.	Sandberg – 97/98	Gordon - .970/.971	Carew: - 3.24
14.	Biggio – 97.97	Collins - .970/.958	Gordon: - 6.48
15.	Hornsby – 95.65	Lazzeri - .967/.968	Gehringer: - 6.48

16. Lazzeri – 92.56	Herman - .967/.966	Morgan: - 11.34
17. McPhee – 92.46	Hornsby - .965/.964	Robinson: - 12.96
18. Lajoie – 84.90	Lajoie - .963/.964	Alomar: - 14.58
19. Collins – 76.76	Evers - .955/.949	Hornsby: - 56.70
20. Evers – 66.55	McPhee - .944/.919	Lazzeri: - 59.94

OBSERVATIONS AND COMMENTARY

Noticeable movements from JAWS to SAWS:

Jackie Robinson moves from 9th to 2nd
Joe Gordon goes from 12th to 6th
Craig Biggio goes from 11th to 17th
Frankie Frisch goes from 7th to 10th
Tony Lazzeri goes from 16th to 11th
Nellie Fox goes from 15th to 19th

Only eight players make the 60% cutoff of 5.87 calculated on the highest score. Twelve players make the cutoff of 60% of the second highest score (4.74) The median is 5.045.

1. Rogers Hornsby – 1915-1937, WAR 1st, JAWS 1st

   Hornsby is the undisputed champion at second base, at least as to offensive statistics. He has seven first place comparative positions including oWAR. He rivals Ted Williams for second place in oWAR overall in the history of baseball. He has the highest right-handed BA at .358 but also packed a home run punch with 301 or 23.2 when season adjusted which is good for second in the room of second basemen. He picked up two MVPs. His dWAR is middle of the pack but the individual comparison categories are erratic. His assists are first but his errors and fielding percentage are seventeenth and his range factor is nineteenth while his double plays are fifteenth. He did spend a considerable amount of his career as a player-manager, so he ended up 70 hits short of 3000. Remarkably he was not selected until his fifth ballot with 78.1%.

2. Jackie Robinson – 1947-1956, WAR 11th, JAWS 9th

   He needs no introduction for breaking the color barrier in Major League Baseball, but he does need considerably more respect as a player than 83rd overall under WAR or 62nd overall under JAWS simply because he played only ten years. He is consistently high in traditional offensive statistics as well as season adjusted statistics putting him fourth in oWAR. He was third in OPB, SLG, OPS, runs created and runs scored. He was sixth in dWAR and first in double plays but poor in range factor. He picked up one MVP out of six considerations and was Rookie of the Year in addition to six All-Star Games. He was a first ballot selection but only with 77.5% of the vote. I would be quite naïve if I thought the low vote count was solely due to a short career and not influenced by race.

3. Eddie Collins – 1906-1930, WAR 2nd, JAWS 2nd

Very strong showing in offensive categories except for home runs and runs batted in as he did lack power. He still came in second in oWAR from being second in OBP, steals, and SO/BB. He was third in BA and fourth in OPS. He was venerable enough to last 25 seasons and still keep his SAWS. Those years gave him the opportunity to accumulate 3315 hits which is eleventh all-time counting Pete Rose. Defensively he was much weaker in comparative stats and sunk all the way to sixteenth in dWAR. He did pick up one MVP, but he also played in the American League in the Twenties. He was also known as the second basemen for the Chicago "Black Sox" in the 1919 World Series who had nothing to do with the "fix." Remarkably he wasn't ordained until his fourth ballot with 77.5% of the vote. Today he would be selected on the first ballot with close to 100%.

4. Napoleon Lajoie – 1896-1916, WAR 3rd, JAWS 3rd

Lajoie was so revered in Cleveland that the team changed its name to the "Naps." He had strong offensive comparisons but much weaker defensive comparisons except for his range factor which was a stunning 92.34 above league per effective season. Overall, he was fifth in oWAR and fourteenth in dWAR. The oWAR ranking is due to second place for BA, fourth place for runs batted in, and fifth place for SLG and OPS. The dWAR comes from eighteenth place in double plays, fielding percentage and errors. He was fairly swift on the bases with almost 26 season adjusted steals which is ninth in the room. Another astounding fact about the writers' vote was that he was not elected until his third ballot with only 83.6%.

5. Joe Morgan – 1963-1984, WAR 4th, JAWS 4th

Joe is one of the marquee names who hung on for as long as possible and weakened noticeably in WAR after the age of 33. But his weakening meant going from 8-9 WAR per season to about 3.5 per season. That dropped him from the 18th greatest overall player under WAR and JAWS to the 25th greatest under SAWS. He had noticeably high offensive comparisons but weaker defensive comparisons. He was third in oWAR but seventeenth in dWAR. He came in first with 46.23 season adjusted steals, but he was also fourth in runs batted in, fifth in home runs, and sixth in OBP. He also collected two MVPs, five Gold Gloves and ten All-Star selections. He came in second for Rookie of the Year. He was an important cog in Cincinnati's "Big Red Machine" of the middle Seventies. He was a first ballot winner with 81.8% of the vote. He was stronger than 81.8% indicates.

6. Joe Gordon – 1938-1950, WAR 12th, JAWS, 12th

My first reaction to this name was "Joe who?" He was the successor to one of the more popular Yankees ever at second base, Tony Lazzeri. He only got in eleven actual seasons due to two years in the military for WWII. His short stay in the majors means he leaps in rank. He was an unassuming slugger with 27.0 season adjusted home runs which is first in this room. Otherwise his oWAR was a weaker rank of twelfth but he was sixth in SLG and eighth in OPS. He was the ranked leader in dWAR with 2.40 season adjusted wins, but the comparative rankings don't illustrate that. He was one percentage point below league fielding average, fifth in double plays, eighth in assists and had a negative range factor. He did pick up one MVP and nine All-Star appointments. Somewhat ignored by the writers for fourteen ballots with a maximum of 28.5% the 2009 Veterans Committee blessed him. Hard to argue with his power and defense.

7. Charlie Gehringer – 1924-1942, WAR 6th, JAWS 5th

Gehirnger is a more balanced player with good offensive comparisons and somewhat weaker defensive comparisons. Seventh in oWAR comes from being second in SLG, OPS and runs created, third in SO/BB ratio, fourth in OBP and fifth in BA and runs batted in. dWAR was a less impressive thirteenth. He picked up one MVP in eleven considerations and six All-Star games after their inception in 1933. He appeared in three World Series and batted a healthy .321. He had one league leadership in BA of .371. Other more esoteric league leaderships were scattered among double, triples, steals, plate appearances, games played, hits and runs scored. He wasn't very glamourous, but he was very effective. He was not voted in until his eighth ballot with 85%.

8. Rod Carew – 1967-1985, WAR 5th, JAWS 6th

A .328 average is hard to ignore but that is Carew's main strength. He had no power but was fifth in OBP and eighth in season adjusted steals, so he held on to sixth in oWAR. His SO/BB ratio is above 1 which is odd for a high average hitter. He also played about half of his career at first base, but it is best to leave him in this room because he would not compare well in that room. Second base or first base, he was a weak fielder. At second he had a fielding percentage four points below league average, last in assists and a negative range factor. He picked up one MVP and eight All-Star games but obviously no Gold Gloves. Comparing him to other approximate.328 hitters like Boggs, Wagner, Lajoie and Collins, he was not impressive at all in SLG, OPS, RBI and SO/BB ratio. A first ballot earner of 90.5% who would not get my vote. Overrated in my opinion.

9. Ryne Sandberg – 1981-1997, WAR 8th, JAWS 7th

One very strange aspect of Sandberg's career is that he retired at 34 years old in 1995 and then returned in 1996 for two more years. He did have a terrible SO/BB ratio coming in at twentieth out of twenty. His best marks were third in homers, seventh in steals and eighth in SLG to rank tenth in oWAR. His dWAR was twelfth but he did have a great fielding percentage of .989. He collected one MVP, eight Gold Gloves, seven Silver Sluggers, and ten All-Star appointments. He was a well-balanced second baseman but not all that famous for anything. It took him until the third ballot with only 76.2% of the vote so even the writers weren't sure about him. Neither am I.

10. Frankie Frisch – 1919-1937, WAR 7th, JAWS 8th

A disparate player with a third place in defense and fourteenth place in oWAR. Offensively he was fifth in runs scored, steals and SO/BB ratio while sixth in BA. Defensively he was second in assists and fifth in range factor with a fielding percentage twelve points above league average. He nabbed one MVP in eight considerations and scattered a few league leaderships around the more peripheral categories. He did land three All-Star appointments after the game began in 1933. He was voted in by the writers on his seventh ballot with 84.5% of the vote. I would venture to say that if the writers knew what he would do on the Veterans Committee from 1967 through 1973 he would not have received 84.5%. Hindsight is 20/20 vision.

11. Tony Lazzeri – 1926-1939, WAR 16th, JAWS 16th

Lazzeri was one of the more popular Yankees when he played with Ruth and Gehrig. He definitely had a little pop in his bat to keep his oWAR at ninth. He was eighth in home runs, second in runs batted in, fourth in SLG and sixth in OPS. He was weaker defensively, fifteenth in dWAR, especially with his range factor where he was dead last. He did pull in one All-Star game after they began in 1933 and was only third in one of his MVP considerations. After fifteen ballots with a maximum of 33.2% of the vote he had to wait until the Veterans Committee of 1991 selected him. Popularity is all well and good, but he lacks too much in the statistical area to qualify in my book. Just a very good second baseman.

12. Roberto Alomar – 1988-2004, WAR 9th, JAWS 10th

Roberto was eighth in oWAR and a distant eighteenth in dWAR. He had some mild pop in his bat. He registered ninth in BA, OBP, SLG, HRs, and runs scored. He was sixth in runs created and eleventh in OPS. He was fourth in stolen bases. He somehow amassed ten Gold Gloves despite his dWAR. His fielding percentage comes in second, but it was only three percentage points above league and his range factor was negative.

He picked up on four Silver Sluggers, and twelve All-Star appointments. His first ballot got him within spitting distance of the Hall with 73.7% and his second ballot put him in with 90%. I cannot see it.

13. Billy Herman – 1931-1947, WAR 13th, JAWS 13th

Herman saw no change from his WAR and JAWS to SAWS. Offensively he is consistently lower than median in comparisons but holds on to thirteenth in oWAR. His only bragging points are eighth in BA and ninth in SO/BB. Defensively he is eleventh in dWAR but around the median. All I could find to tout him was ten All-Star selections. I can push the issue and say he came in third in one of his seven MVP considerations. He led the league in hits, doubles, triples, plate appearances and sacrifice hits once each. He led the league in games played four times. In seven BBWAA votes he went from .8% to 20.2% but did get elected by the Veterans Committee of 1975. I have no idea what they saw in this player. But it was a committee in the Seventies.

14. Bobby Doerr – 1937-1951, WAR 15th, JAWS 14th

Doerr had a little home run punch and achieves fourth in home runs, third in runs batted in and seventh in SLG and OPS. All that makes him fifteenth in oWAR. Defensively his dWAR is ninth but his double plays are third and range factor is fourth. He led the league once each in SLG, triples, grounded into double plays and sacrifice hits. He was also selected for nine All-Star squads. But after fourteen ballots with vote percentages ranging from .08% to 25% he had to wait until the Veterans Committee of 1986 ushered him into the Hall. I am not convinced with Doerr.

15. Johnny Evers – 1902-1917, 1922, 1929, WAR 18th, JAWS 18th

Evers had a good SO/BB ratio and a good ranking for stolen bases, both of which were sixth. Offensively that is it and he is sixteenth in oWAR. His dWAR may be fifth but the individual categories of comparisons indicate lower scores of last in double plays and next to last in fielding percentage but still six points above league average. He did collect one MVP. After eight writers' ballots with rejections he was voted in by the 1946 Old Timers Committee (while being rejected by the writers) along with nine other players including Joe Tinker and Frank Chance. Tinker to Evers to Chance came into the Hall as a group. How disappointing.

16. Bid McPhee – 1882-1899, WAR 14th, JAWS 17th

McPhee was never considered by any writers' vote or any committee until his election in 2000 by the Veterans Committee. I suppose they were paying homage to the early days of baseball. He did steal or advance 568 bases and his SO/BB ratio is strong in fourth place. He was also second in runs scored. Otherwise his offensive comparisons are low, and he is seventeenth in oWAR. When I say low I mean his BA, OPB, OPS, and home runs all come in sixteenth. His SLG is seventeenth and his runs created are eighteenth. His dWAR is slightly above median at eighth and he excelled with a + 81 range factor and a fielding percentage to league of .944 to .919. I just cannot see it, though.

17. Craig Biggio – 1988-2007, WAR 10th, JAWS 11th

Biggio floated around the field from catcher to outfield to second base and landed there for most of his career. His offensive comparisons float around the median with an eleventh at oWAR. There really wasn't much to brag about with his comparison categories other than his sixth rank in home runs and his eighth in runs scored and runs created. His defensive comparisons are not all that impressive, and he is twentieth at dWAR. He is not without other arguments in his favor. He did have 3060 hits, 291 home runs 414 stolen bases, three Gold Gloves, four Silver Sluggers and seven All-Star appointments. The only problem with the awards is that he played twenty seasons. His only league leadership of note is five times being hit by pitches. The writers hesitated with Biggio through three ballots when he finally got 82.7% of the vote. I am still hesitating. 3000 hits are not automatic to me.

18. Red Schoendienst – 1945-1963, WAR 19th, JAWS 19th

Offensively Red is mostly below the median in the comparative statistics and it shows with an oWAR of eighteenth. His highest offensive category is SO/BB where he is eighth. The next highest was his eleventh place BA. His dWAR was seventh in the room and his comparative statistics are clearly above median. He was fourth in double plays, sixth in errors and fifth in fielding percentage being eight percentage points above league average. Other than that, he had ten All-Star selections. One league leadership each in hits and doubles warrants some mention since I am straining to find positives. He suffered through fifteen BBWAA ballots with a maximum of 42.6% before the 1989 Veterans Committee found him. A little plain for my tastes.

19. Nellie Fox – 1947-1965, WAR 17th, JAWS 15th

Fox was quite low offensively in the comparison statistics but at least he was first in SO/BB ratio and twelfth in steals and BA. Defensively he was fourth in dWAR and well above median. He picked up one MVP and twelve All-Star appointments. He even got three Gold Gloves after they were introduced in 1957. From his first ballot with 10.8% to his fifteenth with 74.7% the writers gradually warmed to his defensive skills. The Veterans Committee of 1997 endowed him with fame. This one I can see.

20. Bill Mazeroski – 1956-1972, WAR 20th, JAWS 20th

Let's face it, "Maz" was terrible on offense. He was last in seven offensive categories. His dWAR though was second in the room but he did not take the blue ribbon for any comparative category. He did collect seven All-Star appointments, seven Gold Gloves and managed two MVP considerations but no cigar. He hit one of the most famous home runs in the history of the game in the 1960 World Series to beat the Yankees in the seventh game in the bottom of the ninth. His fifteen ballots scored him from 6.1% to 42.3%. The Veterans Committee of 2001 brought him in. I can see this one as well. Defense at second base has been historically important. It may not stay that way, so it is important to remember the way things were.

THE OTHERS

Jeff Kent's name has been bandied around but all I see is a 4.24 SAWS which would put him sixteenth in the room. His WAR and JAWS would move him up to thirteenth which is below median as well. The 14-17% he is receiving from the BBWAA is about right.

Now that Alan Trammel is in I am sure some are wondering when his teammate, Lou Whitaker will follow. His SAWS is better than Trammell's (5.75 to 5.35) but he amassed all of 2.9% in his first Hall of Fame ballot. I would not bet on him in the committees.

Bobby Grich has a much better SAWS of 6.08 with decent WAR and JAWS numbers of 71.1 and 58.7. He deserves at least as much, if not much more attention as Kent and Whitaker. Maybe the committees need to read this book because he compares to the top third of those in the Hall of Fame now.

SHORTSTOPS

THE SEASONS

	Actual	Total Effective	Effective at SS
1.	Bobby Wallace – 25	14.0981	10.9369
2.	Rabbit Maranville – 23	16.024	12.9993
3.	Honus Wagner – 21	16.6626	11.5165
4.	Cal Ripken – 21	17.9586	13.8765
5.	George Davis – 20	14.0974	8.2610
6.	Robin Yount – 20	16.978	8.8786
7.	Luke Appling – 20	14.1996	13.3987
8.	Joe Cronin – 20	11.8855	11.0192
9.	Alan Trammel – 20	13.2197	12.5309
10.	Ernie Banks – 19	14.7574	6.8265
11.	Ozzie Smith – 19	14.9422	14.9422
12.	Barry Larkin – 19	12.0713	12.0402
13.	Luis Aparicio – 18	15.3695	15.3695
14.	Hughie Jennings – 18	7.5679	5.3594
15.	John Ward – 17	11.273	4.9657
16.	Dave Bancroft – 16	11.3779	11.2805
17.	Pee Wee Reese – 16	12.7588	12.1449
18.	Lou Boudreau – 15	9.6502	9.2483
19.	Joe Tinker – 15	10.706	10.4993
20.	Travis Jackson – 15	9.6756	7.8443
21.	Joe Sewell – 14	11.3121	7.3738
22.	Arky Vaughn – 14	10.3884	8.9479
23.	Phil Rizzuto – 13	9.3653	9.3626

THE RANKINGS

	SAWS	WAR	JAWS
1.	Honus Wagner – 7.86	Wagner – 130.9	Wagner – 98.1
2.	Arky Vaughn – 7.07	Ripken – 95.5	Ripken – 76.1
3.	Lou Boudreau – 6.53	Davis – 84.7	Davis – 64.5
4.	George Davis – 6.01	Yount – 77.3	Yount – 62.3
5.	Barry Larkin – 5.83	Smith – 76.9	Vaughn – 61.8
6.	Hughie Jennings – 5.589	Appling – 74.4	Banks – 59.7
7.	Joe Cronin – 5.586	Vaughn – 72.9	Smith – 59.7
8.	Alan Trammell – 5.35	Trammell – 70.7	Appling – 59.1
9.	Cal Ripken – 5.34	Larkin – 70.4	Trammell – 57.8

10. Luke Appling – 5.24	Wallace – 70.3 (1)	Larkin – 56.9
11. Pee Wee Reese – 5.20	Banks – 67.5	Wallace – 56
12. Ozzie Smith – 5.15	Cronin – 66.4	Boudreau – 55.8
13. Bobby Wallace – 4.99	Reese – 66.3	Cronin – 55.2
14. Joe Tinker – 4.93	Boudreau – 63	Reese – 53.6
15. Joe Sewell – 4.75	Aparicio – 55.8	Sewell – 45.5
16. Ernie Banks – 4.57	Sewell – 53.7	Aparicio – 44.3
17. Robin Yount – 4.553	Tinker – 53.1	Tinker – 43.0
18. Travis Jackson – 4.547	Bancroft – 48.6	Bancroft – 42.9
19. Phil Rizzuto – 4.36	Jackson – 44	Jennings – 40.7
20. Dave Bancroft – 4.27	Maranville – 42.9	Jackson – 39.5
21. Luis Aparicio – 3.63	Jennings – 42.3	Rizzuto – 37.3
22. John Ward – 3.58	Rizzuto – 40.8	Maranville – 36.7
23. Rabbit Maranville – 2.67	Ward – 34.3(2)	Ward – 29.5

(1) Wallace also has a pitching WAR of 6.2 in addition to the WAR at Shortstop

(2) Ward also has a pitching WAR of 28.4 in addition to the WAR at Shortstop

THE OFFENSIVE COMPARISONS

	BA	OBP	SLG	OPS
1.	Wagner - .328	Vaughn - .406	Banks - .500	Vaughn - .859
2.	Vaughn - .318	Appling - .399	Cronin - .468	Wagner - .858
3.	Sewell - .3121	Wagner - .3911	Wagner - .467	Cronin - .857
4.	Jennings - .3117	Sewell - .3909	Vaughn - .453	Banks - .830
5.	Appling - .310	Jennings - .3907	Ripken - .447	Larkin - .815
6.	Cronin - .301	Cronin - .390	Larkin - .444	Sewell - .804
7.	Boudreau - .2951	Boudreau - .380	Jackson - .443	Appling - .798
8.	Larkin - .2948	Larkin - .371	Yount - .430	Jennings - .797
9.	Davis - .2946	Reese - .366	Trammell - .4153	Boudreau - .795
10.	Jackson - .291	Davis - .362	Boudreau - .4147	Ripken - .788
11.	Trammell - .2854	Bancroft -.355	Sewell - .413	Yount - .772
12.	Yount - .2854	Trammell - .352	Jennings - .406	Jackson - .770
13.	Bancroft - .279	Rizzuto - .351	Davis - .405	Trammell - .7668
14.	Ripken - .276	Yount - .342	Appling - .388	Davis - .7666
15.	Ward - .275	Ripken - .340	Reese - .377	Reese - .743
16.	Banks - .274	Smith - .3375	Wallace - .358	Bancroft - .714
17.	Rizzuto - .273	Jackson - .337	Bancroft - .358	Rizzuto - .706
18.	Reese - .269	Wallace - .332	Rizzuto - .355	Wallace - .690

19.	Wallace - .268	Banks - .330	Tinker - .353	Smith - .666
20.	Tinker - .2624	Maranville - .318	Aparicio - .343	Tinker - .661
21.	Smith - .2618	Ward - .314	Ward - .341	Maranville - .658
22.	Aparicio - .2617	Aparicio - .311	Maranville - .340	Ward - .655
23.	Maranville. - .258	Tinker - .308	Smith - .328	Aparicio - .653

	oWAR/162	Runs Created/162	SO/BB Ratio	Steals/162
1.	Wagner – 7.39	Vaughn – 117.05	Sewell - .1354	Ward – 47.90
2.	Vaughn – 6.83	Cronin – 115.27	Vaughn - .2946	Jennings – 47.43
3.	Larkin – 5.65	Larkin – 114.4	Boudreau - .3882	Davis – 43.48
4.	Cronin – 5.37	Wagner – 113.31	Appling - .4132	Wagner – 43.39
5.	Boudreau – 5.22	Banks – 102.46	Smith - .5494	Smith – 38.82
6.	Jennings – 5.03	Sewell – 99.54	Bancroft - .5889	Aparicio – 32.92
7.	Davis – 5.02	Appling – 99.44	Rizzuto - .6114	Larkin – 31.4
8.	Appling – 4.97	Boudreau – 97.72	Cronin - .6610	Tinker – 31.22
9.	Yount – 4.89	Yount – 97.48	Jennings - .6744	Reese – 18.18
10.	Sewell – 4.773	Jennings – 96.99	Davis - .7014	Maranville – 18.16
11.	Trammell – 4.766	Ripken – 96.28	Wallace - .7261	Trammell – 17.85
12.	Reese – 4.37	Trammell – 94.94	Reese - .7355	Yount – 15.96
13.	Ripken – 4.35	Davis – 94.56	Wagner - .7632	Rizzuto – 15.91
14.	Banks – 4.21	Jackson – 92.09	Ward - .7743	Wallace – 14.26
15.	Wallace – 4.02	Reese – 88.17	Larkin - .8701	Bancroft – 12.74
16.	Bancroft – 3.45	Bancroft – 79.89	Maranville - .9011	Appling – 12.61
17.	Smith – 3.27	Rizzuto – 78.27	Aparicio – 1.0082	Vaughn – 11.36
18.	Jackson – 3.18	Smith – 77.36	Trammell – 1.0282	Jackson – 7.34
19.	Tinker – 3.05	Aparicio – 73.85	Ripken – 1.16	Cronin – 7.32
20.	Rizzuto – 3.04	Ward – 73.18	Tinker – 1.2644	Sewell – 6.54
21.	Aparicio – 2.75	Wallace – 72.7	Jackson – 1.3714	Boudreau – 5.31
22.	Ward – 2.63	Maranville – 68.58	Yount – 1.3945	Banks – 3.39
23.	Maranville – 1.86	Tinker – 65.38	Banks – 1.6199	Ripken – 2.00

	HR/162	RBI/162	RunsScored/162
1.	Banks – 34.67	Cronin – 119.81	Jennings – 131.08
2.	Ripken – 24.0	Jennings – 111.0	Ward – 125.08
3.	Larkin – 16.4	Banks – 110.86	Vaughn – 112.91
4.	Yount – 14.78	Wagner – 103.95	Davis – 109.59
5.	Cronin – 14.30	Davis – 102.15	Wagner – 104.37
6.	Trammell – 14.0	Jackson – 96.01	Sewell – 100.87
7.	Jackson – 13.95	Ripken – 94.38	Yount – 96.12

8. Reese – 9.88	Sewell – 93.17	Reese – 94.85
9. Vaughn – 9.24	Boudreau – 89.22	Rizzuto – 93.64
10. Boudreau – 7.05	Vaughn – 89.14	Trammell – 93.13
11. Wagner – 6.06	Yount – 82.81	Bancroft – 92.11
12. Aparacio – 5.40	Wallace – 79.51	Ripken – 91.71
13. Davis – 5.18	Larkin – 79.53	Appling – 91.69
14. Sewell – 4.33	Appling – 78.59	Cronin – 89.10
15. Rizzuto – 4.06	Ward – 77.09	Banks – 88.43
16. Appling – 3.17	Trammell – 75.88	Aparicio – 86.86
17. Tinker – 2.90	Tinker – 73.32	Jackson – 86.09
18. Bancroft – 2.81	Reese – 69.37	Smith – 84.12
19. Wallace – 2.41	Rizzuto – 60.12	Boudreau – 82.49
20. Jennings – 2.38	Maranville – 55.17	Maranville – 78.38
21. Ward – 2.31	Smith – 53.07	Larkin – 77.79
22. Smith – 1.87	Bancroft – 51.94	Wallace – 74.97
23. Maranville – 1.75	Aparicio – 51.47	Tinker – 72.30

THE DEFENSIVE COMPARISONS

dWAR/162	Assists/162	Errors/162
1. Tinker – 3.20	Jackson - 591	Ripken – 16.21
2. Smith – 2.96	Jennings – 586.45	Trammell – 18.12
3. Rizzuto – 2.45	Bancroft – 581.62	Smith – 18.81
4. Boudreau – 2.425	Davis – 580.32	Larkin – 19.52
5. Jackson – 2.37	Wallace – 576.31	Aparicio – 23.81
6. Aparicio – 2.069	Maranvillle – 565.72	Boudreau – 24.11
7. Bancroft – 2.065	Smith – 560.49	Banks – 25.49
8. Wallace – 2.04	Tinker – 557. 76	Rizzuto – 28.09
9. Reese – 2.01	Yount – 539.95	Yount – 30.64
10. Ripken – 1.99	Appling – 538.71	Reese – 31.95
11. Maranville – 1.92	Vaughn – 534.20	Cronin – 44.04
12. Trammell – 1.72	Sewell – 533.38	Vaughn – 44.37
13. Davis – 1.702	Ward – 531.85	Sewell – 45.16
14. Appling – 1.34	Cronin – 527.62	Appling – 47.99
15. Wagner – 1.28	Wagner – 524.55	Maranville – 48.54
16. Cronin – 1.20	Aparicio – 521.55	Jackson – 48.57
17. Larkin – 1.19	Boudreau – 514.69	Bancroft – 58.51
18. Jennings – 1.19	Banks – 504.06	Wagner – 58.70
19. Vaughn – 1.15	Ripken – 502.79	Tinker – 60.48

20. Ward - .923	Rizzuto – 498.37	Davis – 61.86
21. Sewell - .804	Trammel – 492.54	Wallace – 62.63
22. Yount - .401 (1)	Reese – 485.06	Jennings – 103
23. Banks - .346 (2)	Larkin – 486.54	Ward – 106.73

(1) Yount's dWAR is for both shortstop and centerfield, Separately as SS he had a season adjusted dWAR of approximately 1.47.
(2) Banks' dWAR is for both shortstop and first base. Separately he had a season adjusted dWAR of approximately1.83 at SS.

Double Plays/162	FP/162 to League	RF/162 to League
1. Rizzuto – 129.99	Ripken - .979/.969	Jennings: + 95.98
2. Boudreau – 127.59	Smith - .978/.966	Smith: + 71.28
3. Ripken – 112.78	Trammell - .977/.967	Bancroft: + 68.04
4. Smith – 106.41	Larkin - .975/.968	Wallace: + 46.98
5. Appling – 106.28	Boudreau - .973/.954	Maranville: + 46.98
6. Banks – 106.06	Aparicio - .972/.963	Davis: + 45.36
7. Yount – 105.99	Banks - .969/.962	Wagner: + 42.12
8. Cronin – 105.72	Rizzuto - .968/.959	Tinker: + 42.12
9. Jackson – 105.30	Yount - .964/.964	Sewell: + 38.88
10. Trammell – 104.30	Reese - .962/.958	Yount: + 37.26
11. Reese – 102.59	Jackson - .952/.949	Jackson: + 35.64
12. Aparicio – 101.04	Maranville - .952/.940	Aparicio: + 25.92
13. Vaughn – 94.99	Sewell - .951/.944	Appling: + 22.68
14. Maranville – 91.39	Vaughn - .951/.949	Rizzuto: + 21.46
15. Sewell – 91.27	Cronin - .951/.946	Ward: + 16.20
16. Larkin – 90.70	Appling - .948/.952	Cronin: + 12.96
17. Bancroft – 90.51	Bancroft - .944/.941	Larkin: + 8.10
18. Jennings – 76.69	Wagner - .940/.927	Ripken: + 6.48
19. Davis – 71.42	Davis - .940/.923	Banks: 0
20. Wagner – 66.51	Tinker - .938/.926	Boudreau: -1.62
21. Tinker – 63.91	Wallace - .938/.926	Trammell: - 9.72
22. Ward – 59.21	Jennings - .922/.900	Reese: - 11.34
23. Wallace – 58.52	Ward - .887/.880	Vaughn: - 11.34

OBSERVATIONS AND COMMENTARY

Noticeable moves from JAWS to SAWS:

Ernie Banks goes from 6th to 16th

Robin Yount goes from 4th to 17th
Ozzie Smith goes from 7th to 12th
Hughie Jennings goes from 19th to 5th
Lou Boudreau goes from 12th to 3rd
Cal Ripken goes from 2nd to 9th

Fifteen players make the 60% cutoff of 4.716. The median is Ozzie Smith at 5.15

1. Honus Wagner – 1897-1917, WAR 1st, JAWS 1st

   He is first in WAR, JAWS and SAWS and he played a full 21-year career. There is no short career to elevate him. He is an example of quantity and quality. That is why he was one of the "Five Immortals" first chosen for the Hall of Fame in 1936. He walks away with first in oWAR and the comparisons back him up. He was first in BA, second in OPS, third in OBP and SLG, fourth in runs created, runs batted in and stolen bases and fifth in runs scored. His dWAR falls to fifteenth though, but he had good range at + 42 and thirteen percentage points above league fielding average. He had 30 league leaderships in the main categories of batting and was sixth in dominance ranking. He had 3420 hits and stole 723 bases. You can probably consider him the first superstar of the modern era beginning in 1901.

2. Arky Vaughn – 1932-1948, WAR 7th, JAWS 5th

   Vaughn moves up a few spots from JAWS and WAR due to his offensive prowess coupled with a short career. He was second in oWAR and noticeably in the top layers of offensive comparison statistics including first in OBP, OPS and runs created, second in BA and SO/BB ratio, third in runs and fourth in SLG. Not so high though with dWAR as he falls to nineteenth and the statistics concur. He was eleventh in assists, thirteenth in double plays, two percentage points below league average in fielding and last in range factor. He found his way to nine All-Star games and had three league leaderships in OPB and one each in BA, SLG and OPS. He came in third on two of seven MVP ballots. According to Ralph Moses of SABR BioProject Arky had a dispute with management, threatened a players' strike and sat out for three years. His BBWAA ballots totaled thirteen with votes ranging from .4% to 29%. He was forced to wait until the Veterans Committee of 1985 met to elect him. I am uncomfortable with him because of his very poor fielding statistics for a shortstop but he does have the numbers offensively. In fact, those numbers are what makes him the 20th greatest player under SAWS.

3. Lou Boudreau – 1938-1952, WAR 14th, JAWS 12th

   I can attribute his elevated status to a short but high quality playing career where the number of games played fell due to managerial duties with the Cleveland Indians. He comes in fifth in oWAR thanks to third in SO/BB, seventh in BA and OBP, eighth in OPS and runs created, ninth in SLG and runs batted in and tenth in homers. His dWAR is fourth despite a ranking of twentieth in range factor and only one percentage point above league fielding percentage. He was second in double plays, though. He picked up one MVP out of ten considerations and seven All-Star assignments. I can live with it.

4. George Davis – 1890-1909, WAR 3rd, JAWS 3rd

I found out when comparing JAWS and SAWS that George Davis and Joe DiMaggio are tied in 33rd place overall under JAWS. Anomalies exist, and you will see them in SAWS as well. Overall his oWAR is seventh which indicates good offensive abilities. His rankings include third in stolen bases, fourth in runs scored, fifth in runs batted in, ninth in BA, tenth in OBP and SO/BB, and thirteenth in home runs, SLG and runs created. His dWAR was thirteenth, though, but he did have a positive range factor of 45 above league average and a good fielding percentage compared to league average. He played in one World Series and batted .308. He did lead the league in RBI one year. He finished his career before awards and accolades came to pass. He was totally ignored by everyone until the 1998 Veterans Committee plucked him out of nowhere. I must rely on numbers and leave him in as WAR and JAWS rate him third so there is sufficient agreement as to quality. He still isn't the equivalent of DiMaggio.

5. Barry Larkin – 1986-2004, WAR 9th, JAWS 10th

He is third in oWAR and except for runs scored and runs batted in he is in the top layers of offensive comparisons. Those comparisons include third in runs created and home runs, fifth in OPS, sixth in SLG, seventh in stolen bases and eighth in BA and OBP. He tumbles to seventeenth in dWAR and a low range factor of + 8 is noted as well as dead last in assists. He corralled one MVP in six votes in addition to three Gold Gloves, nine Silver Sluggers and twelve All-Star appointments. He batted .353 in one World Series. The writers were hesitant and did not vote him in until his third ballot and then with only 86.4% of the vote. I think the third ballot is where I might have come around to voting for him. The operative word is "might."

6. Hughie Jennings – 1891-1903, 1908-1910, 1912, 1918, WAR 21st, JAWS 19th

Jennings had the least number of effective seasons for a shortstop at 7.57 but that is about the same amount Jackie Robinson had so you can display excellence in a short career. He frequents the higher positions in comparative statistics offensively and his oWAR comes in sixth. Those higher positions include first in runs scored, second in stolen bases and runs batted in, fourth in BA and fifth in OBP, eighth in OPS, ninth in SO/BB, tenth in runs created, and twelfth in SLG. His dWAR falls to eighteenth but he had a great number of assists (second place) due to his fantastic range (first place) . He actually batted .401 which may be the only shortstop to ever do so. He also holds a career record of being hit by pitches 287 times. After six ballots from the BBWAA with 2% - 37% of the vote the 1945 Old Timers Committee chose him while the writers in 1945 were rejecting him. I think he is a keeper. I am sure he would be yelling ee-yah right now.

7. Joe Cronin – 1926-1945, WAR 12th, JAWS 13th

He is above the median in comparative statistics offensively and occasionally hovers around the top but his defensive play is not rated that good. He is fourth in oWAR and sixteenth in dWAR. Offensively he is first in runs batted in, second in SLG, third in OPS, fifth in home runs, sixth in BA and OBP, and eighth in SO/BB. He had a range factor of +16 but that is sixteenth place. He rounded up seven All-Star appointments and came in second in one of his eight MVP considerations. He stayed on eleven writers' ballots climbing from 3.7% to 78.8% in 1956, the same year he was chosen American League President. I'm suspicious.

8. Alan Trammell – 1977-1996, WAR 8th, JAWS 9th

His offensive comparisons, other than home runs where he is sixth, track more closely with the median rather than eighth. Specifically, he is ninth in SLG, tenth in runs scored, eleventh in BA and stolen bases, twelfth in OBP and runs created, thirteenth in OPS, sixteenth in runs batted in and eighteenth in SO/BB. His defensive statistics are up and down. He is second in all-time fielding percentage at shortstop but 21st in range factor. Overall, he is eleventh in oWAR and twelfth in dWAR. He had no league leaderships and only fourth in the Rookie of the Year balloting. In twenty years he only scratched out three Gold Gloves and three Silver Sluggers. His best MVP vote was second in seven considerations and he only saw six All-Star selections. He stayed on the ballot for the full fifteen years scaling to a 40.9%. In 2018 the Veterans Committee smiled upon him. He seems much more middle of the road than even an eight rank indicates. Questionable as to fame as well.

9. Cal Ripken – 1981-2001, WAR 2nd, JAWS 2nd

His season adjusted oWAR comes in thirteenth and his dWAR comes in tenth and his individual comparisons do not produce a counterargument. His career dWAR is fourth all time, though. Statistics and rankings are fine but with Ripken they are not as important. He played in 3001 games and only eight have played in more. He played in 2632 of those games consecutively besting Lou Gehrig's record which had stood since the 1930s. He collected 3184 hits and the Rookie of the Year designation. He collected two MVPs, one Gold Glove, seven Silver Sluggers, and nineteen All-Star appointments. He was a first ballot selection with 98.5% of the vote.

10. Luke Appling – 1930-1950, WAR 6th, JAWS 8th

His SAWS shows him tenth but his oWAR is eighth and his dWAR is fourteenth. His rankings are an olio of numbers. He was second in OBP, fourth in SO/BB, fifth in BA, seventh in OPS and runs created, thirteenth in runs scored, fourteenth in SLG and RBI, and sixteenth in stolen bases and home runs. Defensive rankings include fifth in double plays, tenth in assists, thirteenth in range factor and sixteenth in fielding percentage. He led the league in BA twice and in OBP once. He amassed 2749 hits, which ranks 56th in career numbers, but he lost one year to WWII. When it comes to MVP he comes in second twice in eleven considerations. In eight ballots he went from .8% to 94% in a runoff ballot where only one was selected.

11. Pee Wee Reese – 1940-1958, WAR 13th, JAWS 14th

Missing three years to WWII at the ages of 24, 25, and 26 are important to note as it is the reason for lower career numbers as well as WAR and JAWS. His oWAR slips a rank to twelfth but his dWAR rises to ninth. He was eighth in home runs and runs scored, ninth in OBP and stolen bases, fifteenth in SLG and OPS and eighteenth in BA and RBI. Defensively he was 22nd in range factor and assists, and tenth in fielding percentage and eleventh in double plays. He was considered for MVP status thirteen times in his sixteen seasons but never finished higher than fifth. He was the unmistakable captain of the Dodgers in the 1950s and appeared in seven World Series. He had image but not the greatest numbers. After fifteen ballots the writers rejected him with a maximum of 47.9% but the Veterans Committee of 1984 remedied that wrong.

12. Ozzie Smith – 1978-1996, WAR 5th, JAWS 7th

He was tremendously weak offensively. His high marks were fifth in stolen bases and SO/BB ratio. Moving way down the chart to sixteenth is his OBP. After that comes eighteenth in runs created and runs scored, nineteenth in OPS, 21st in BA and RBI, 22nd in home runs, and 23rd in SLG. Defensively his season adjusted dWAR came in second to Tinker. He was second in range factor with a +71.28 which is rarely seen in modern day shortstops. Defense was his forte. Playing a little on the longer side did drop him from fifth in WAR and seventh in JAWS. Fifteen All-Star games, thirteen Gold Gloves, one Silver Slugger and a vote of second in one of his six MVP considerations. The BBWAA showed its respect for fielding with a 91.7% first ballot vote.

13. Bobby Wallace – 1894-1918, WAR 10th, JAWS 11th

Noting the 25-year career it should be known that he only played 144 games in his last six years as he managed. Offensively his comparison numbers run from median to well below median and land at fifteenth in oWAR. To be precise his best two are eleventh in SO/BB and fourteenth in stolen bases. He sinks lower to sixteenth in SLG and eighteenth is the home for OBP and OPS. Then comes BA and home runs at nineteenth. Runs created comes in at 21st and runs scored comes in at 22nd. His dWAR comes in eighth and he did have very good range at +46.98. He had a career dWAR of 28.7 which puts him 10th in the career history books. With six ballots from the writers he went from .5 to 2.7%. The Veterans Committee of 1953 may be the first to recognize fielding ability because he sure was lacking in offense.

14. Joe Tinker – 1902-1916, WAR 17th, JAWS 17th

He is the #1 shortstop in season adjusted dWAR and fifth in career dWAR. He was moderately adept at stealing bases and possessed a good range factor. There is nothing else all that positive to say. Seriously, he was seventeenth in home runs and runs batted in, nineteenth in SLG and oWAR, twentieth in BA and SO/BB, 23rd in runs scored, runs created and OBP. He was actually 21st in season adjusted double plays! But the rhythmic chant of "Tinker to Evers to Chance" must have mesmerized the Old Timers Committee of 1946 especially since the writers had rejected him on seven ballots. He is the best of the three but that is not saying much.

15. Joe Sewell – 1920-1933, WAR 16th, JAWS 15th

Sewell is atypical for a shortstop. His oWAR goes to tenth while his dWAR goes to 21st. His main claim to fame is a SO/BB ratio of .1354. Stated another way that is one strikeout per 62.56 at bats and second only to Willie Keeler. But he had a myriad of different rankings. Third in BA and fourth in OBP are merely a precursor to sixth in runs created and runs scored and eighth in RBI. Next up was eleventh in SLG and fourteenth in home runs. Last was twentieth in stolen bases. His dWAR rankings were mixed. He was twelfth in assists, fifteenth in double plays, thirteenth in fielding percentage with seven percentage points above league average. Finally, his range factor above league was ninth at +38. He had a consecutive game played streak of 1103 games. He came in third in seven MVP votes. As to BBWAA votes he also had seven ballots where he ranged from .4% – 8.6%. The Veterans Committee of 1977 picked him out of the crowd. Why?

16. Ernie Banks – 1953-1971, WAR 11th, JAWS 6th

His oWAR comes in at fourteenth despite 512 career home runs and season adjusted figure of 34.67 which is tied for 23rd all-time and 27th all-time respectively. Compared to other 500 home run hitters such as Mantle, Schmidt, Mathews, Murray, Ott, Thomas and Foxx he comes in at or close to the bottom for OPB, SLG, OPS+, runs scored and SO/BB ratio. The rest of his offensive rankings at shortstop are mixed. His dWAR at shortstop is respectable and almost median but that is not the major point to discuss. Offensively Banks was basically one dimensional. He hit home runs. He had no speed on the bases as he successfully stole 50 bases and was caught stealing 53 times – in his career. He did not hit for average with a .274. Only Yount has more season adjusted errors for a more modern-day player and Banks had a 0-range factor above league. He came in last with his SO/BB ratio. He did collect two MVPs primarily for hitting home runs as well as eleven All-Star appointments. He was a first ballot selection with 83.8% of the vote meaning 62 writers did not put a check mark next to his name. I would not have either despite the image and name recognition. Maybe in a later ballot…and maybe not.

17. <u>Robin Yount – 1974-1993, WAR 4th, JAWS 4th</u>

Yount was a long-term Milwaukee Brewer fan favorite who accumulated 3142 hits, albeit with the aid of 137 DH games. His oWAR came up to ninth and he was all over the place with the individual rankings and his dWAR at short came up to slightly above median, but he did make a lot of errors for a modern-day shortstop. The offensive rankings look like this: fourth in home runs, seventh in runs scored, eighth in SLG, ninth in runs created, eleventh in OPS and RBI, twelfth in BA and stolen bases, fourteenth in OBP and 22nd in SO/BB. His defensive rankings are ninth in assists, seventh in double plays, ninth in fielding percentage but only matching the league average, and tenth in range factor at +37. He did receive two MVPs one at shortstop and one in centerfield, but MVPs usually relate to offense, not a position. He got one Gold Glove and two Silver Sluggers at shortstop and one more Silver Slugger in centerfield. He only received three All-Star selections in twenty years. He led the league once in SLG and OPS once, so you cannot call him dominant. He was elected on the first ballot with 77.5%. He would not have had my vote as I think the 3000+ hits did the trick for him and that is not an automatic qualifier for me. It is too longevity connected especially with a .285 BA.

18. <u>Travis Jackson – 1922-1936, WAR 19th, JAWS 20th</u>

This was one of the most unfamiliar names I ran across when delving into this project. His dWAR was excellent and in fifth place and he ranked first in assists, ninth in double plays, and eleventh in range factor (+37) and fielding percentage (three percentage points above league). His offense has some good points, some not so good points and some in between. At the top of the list was sixth in RBI. Then came home runs and SLG at seventh. Next was twelfth in OPS and fourteenth in runs created. Continuing our descent, he comes in seventeenth in runs scored and OBP and eighteenth in stolen bases and oWAR. Finally, he checks in at 21st in SO/BB. He placed fourth in one of seven MVP considerations and got one All-Star appointment in 1934. Twelve writers' ballots showered him with all of .6% to 4.1% of the votes.

Then the 1982 Veterans Committee found something to justify enshrining him. I don't know what that was, but I am sure it wasn't image. The only thing I can speculate to is a greater appreciation of defense.

19. Phil Rizzuto – 1941-1956 WAR 22nd, JAWS 21st

Rizzuto is another shortstop who loses three years to WWII and ends up with only thirteen seasons. Following a familiar pattern, he has a oWAR of 20th and a third place for dWAR. Remarkably not a single offensive comparative category of his drops to twentieth. He was seventh in SO/BB, ninth in runs scored, thirteenth in stolen bases with a fifteenth spot in home runs. OPS and runs created came in seventeenth while RBI brought up the rear at nineteenth. He was first in double plays and eighth in fielding percentage with nine percentage points above league. This was the typical shortstop in baseball history, but I fear the game has changed in that very soon bad defense will be tolerated with better offense. So be it. "Scooter" landed one MVP in eight reviews and five All-Star appointments. In sixteen BBWAA ballots he rose up to 38% and found victory in the Veterans Committee of 1994. I can live with this.

20. Dave Bancroft – 1915-1930, WAR 18th, JAWS 18th

His oWAR edges up a little from his SAWS ranking to sixteenth thanks to a thirteen for BA, an eleven for OPB and runs scored. Throw in a sixth place for SO/BB and sixteenth for runs created and OPS just for good measure. His dWAR is strong at seven due to a great range factor (third place and + 68 plays) and first in assists. He was sixth and ninth in two MVP votes and led the league once in games played. My laudatory comments end there. After fifteen BBWAA ballots ranging from 3.3% to 16.2% the 1971 Veterans Committee reared its ugly head (again) with this choice.

21. Luis Aparicio – 1956-1973, WAR 15th, JAWS 16th

Another typical, low season oWAR and high dWAR. The former being 21st in the room and the latter being sixth. The comparative statistics concur and are very commonplace for both. He also had 506 SB which adjusts to 32.92 for sixth in the room. He led the league nine times in stolen bases. He also won Rookie of the Year, had ten All-Star appointments and was considered for ten MVPs coming in second once. His defense earned him nine Gold Gloves as his career dWAR reached 31.8 as the sixth highest in baseball history. Finally, after six ballots the writers relented and gave him 84.6% of the vote in 1984. It was about time the BBWAA recognized defense.

22. John M. Ward. – 1878-1894 WAR 23rd, JAWS 23rd

Ward is equally balanced in oWAR and dWAR as well as SAWS, all in 22nd place. Solely as a shortstop he has no business being in the Hall of Fame. Add in his pitching WAR and that is a different story. The 1936 Veterans Committee shrugged him off with 3.8% of the vote. The 1964 Veterans Committee sang a different tune and elected him. It could have been deference to 19th century players or it could have been something in the water at the meeting. Bill Lamb and his SABR BioProject on John Montgomery Ward has considerably more information about this player and his pioneering place in baseball. As a player though he is a mixed bag. But it is hard to ignore his total WAR when pitching WAR is included.

23. Rabbit Maranville – 1912-1935, WAR 20th, JAWS 22nd

At 5'5" and 155 lbs. he wasn't much bigger than a rabbit. There is no sense in belaboring the offensive placements. They all are twentieth or lower. He owns the room's worst season adjusted oWAR but climbs up to eleventh in dWAR. His career dWAR was 30.8 and ranks seventh all-time. He had his best marks in range factor and assists which is not unusual to see those two stats go hand in hand. His BA rivals Harmon Killebrew (.256) and Ray Schalk (.253) for last place. He placed and showed in eight MVP considerations. After sixteen ballots he climbed to 82.9% in 1954. He did have an image and that is probably what got him in. I can live with it. But then again, I like defense.

THE OTHERS

Derek Jeter in 2020 will probably revive all the silly talk we heard with Ken Griffey about a unanimous vote into the Hall. If I were a voting writer Jeter would be missing my vote. The main reason would be the career dWAR of - 8.6. A shortstop should be at least a good fielder. He was not. It is that simple. And if you look at his WAR of 72.4, JAWS of 57.4 and SAWS of 4.42 his rank in this room of shortstops would be 8th, 10th and 19th respectively. His quantity did not affect his quality as adversely as others. Yes, he should be in the Hall of Fame...but he is not 100% perfect.

Omar Vizquel has weak WAR of 45.6, JAWS of 36.2 and SAWS of 2.89 which puts him close to the bottom in the rankings. His career dWAR of 29.5 is impressive, though.

The name Bill Dahlen comes up occasionally and he sports a 75.4 WAR, a 57.8 JAWS and a 5.14 SAWS with a career dWAR of 28.5. Note that those are all better than Jeter. A committee needs to rectify this situation.

Mark Belanger has the highest season adjusted dWAR in all of baseball with a 3.725 but I can assure you he will never be in the Hall of Fame with a .228 BA. oWAR and dWAR were not created equally. Wow...can you just imagine Brooks Robinson, Mark Belanger and Bobby Grich in your infield?

LEFTFIELDERS

THE SEASONS

	Actual	Total Effective	Effective in LF
1.	Rickey Henderson – 25	17.1562	13.6078
2.	Carl Yastrzemski – 23	19.4419	11.3004
3.	Jim O'Rourke – 23	12.1337	8.6735
4.	Tim Raines – 23	13.5771	11.1993
5.	Willie Stargell – 21	12.316	7.1175
6.	Fred Clarke – 21	13.2037	13.1680
7.	Al Simmons – 20	12.8464	12.8409
8.	Ted Williams – 19	12.5107	12.509
9.	Lou Brock – 19	14.7410	12.6774
10.	Zack Wheat – 19	14.1337	17.8786
11.	Goose Goslin – 18	13.1036	13.096
12.	Billy Williams – 18	14.6596	10.193
13.	Heine Manush – 17	10.9396	10.9369
14.	Joe Kelley – 17	10.6948	8.8213
15.	Joe Medwick – 17	11.1687	11.0761
16.	Ed Delahanty – 16	11.1235	8.1379
17.	Jesse Burkett – 16	12.5021	12.4033
18.	Jim Rice – 16	12.5560	9.0252
19.	Chick Hafey – 13	7.0741	7.0741
20.	Ralph Kiner – 10	8.5562	6.4689

THE RANKINGS

	SAWS	WAR	JAWS
1.	Ted Williams – 9.84	T Williams – 123.1	T Williams – 96.1
2.	Rickey Henderson – 6.48	Henderson – 111.2	Henderson – 84.4
3.	Ed Delahanty – 6.266	Yastrzemski – 96.4	Yastrzemski – 75.9
4.	Ralph Kiner – 5.77	Delahanty – 69.7	Delahanty – 59.1
5.	Al Simmons – 5.36	Raines – 69.4	Simmons – 57.3
6.	Fred Clarke – 5.14	Simmons – 68.8	Raines – 55.9
7.	Tim Raines – 5.11	Clarke – 67.9	Goslin – 54.7
8.	Goose Goslin – 5.04	Goslin – 66.1	B Williams – 52.6
9.	Jesse Burkett – 5.02	B Williams – 63.7	Clarke – 52.1
10.	Joe Medwick – 4.98	Burkett – 62.7	Burkett – 49.9
11.	Carl Yastrzemski – 4.96	Wheat – 60.2	Stargell – 47.7
12.	Joe Kelley – 4.74	Stargell – 57.5	Medwick – 47.7

13. Willie Stargell – 4.67	Medwick – 55.6	Wheat – 47.4
14. Billy Williams – 4.35	O'Rourke – 51.5	Kiner – 46.5
15. Zack Wheat – 4.259	Kelley – 50.7	Kelley – 43.5
16. Chick Hafey – 4.255	Kiner – 49.4	Rice – 42.1
17. Jim O'Rourke – 4.24	Rice – 47.7	Manush – 40.2
18. Heinie Manush – 4.11	Manush – 45.8	Brock – 38.7
19. Jim Rice – 3.80	Brock – 45.3	O'Rourke – 37.9
20. Lou Brock – 3.07	Hafey – 30.1	Hafey – 28.6

THE OFFENSIVE CATEGORIES

	BA	OBP	SLG	OPS
1.	Delahanty - .346	T Williams - .482	T Williams - .634	T Williams – 1.116
2.	T Williams - .344	Burkett - .415	Kiner - .548	Kiner - .946
3.	Burkett - .338	Delahanty - .411	Simmons - .535	Delahanty - .916
4.	Simmons - .334	Kelley - .402	Stargell - .529	Simmons - .915
5.	Manush - .330	Henderson - .401	Hafey - .526	Hafey - .898
6.	Medwick - .324	Kiner - .398	Delahanty - .5052	Stargell - .889
7.	Hafey - .3170	Clarke - .396	Medwick – 504.5	Goslin - .887
8.	Kelley - .3169	Goslin - .387	Rice - .502	Medwick - .867
9.	Wheat - .3167	Raines - .385	Goslin - .500	Burkett - .861
10.	Goslin - .3160	Simmons - .380	B Williams - .492	Manush - .856
11.	Clarke - .312	Yastrzemski - .379	Manush - .479	Rice - .854
12.	O'Rourke - .310	Manush - .377	Yastrzemski - .462	B Williams - .8533
13.	Rice - .298	Hafey - .372	Kelley - .451	Kelley - .8529
14.	Raines - .294	Wheat - .367	Wheat - .450	Yastrzemski - .841
15.	Brock - .293	Medwick - .362	Burkett - .446	Wheat - .827
16.	B Williams - .290	B Williams - .361	Clarke - .429	Henderson - .820
17.	Yastrzemski - .285	Stargell- .360	Raines - .425	Clarke - .814
18.	Stargell - .282	O'Rourke - .3522	O'Rourke - .422	Raines - .810
19.	Kiner - .2788	Rice - .3519	Henderson - .419	O'Rourke - .775
20.	Henderson - .2787	Brock - .343	Brock - .410	Brock - .753

	Runs Scored/162	Runs Created/162	OPS+	SO/BB Ratio
1.	Delahanty – 143.84	T Williams – 190.4	T Williams – 190	T Williams - .3524
2.	T Williams – 143.72	Delahanty – 141.41	B Williams – 153	Kelley - .4720
3.	O'Rourke – 142.5	Simmons – 139.18	Delahanty – 152	Clarke - .5840
4.	Burkett – 137.58	Kiner – 133.7	Kiner – 149	Delahanty - .5924
5.	Henderson – 133.17	Hafey – 127.7	Stargell – 147	Burkett - .5957

6.	Kelley – 132.87	Goslin – 127.22	Burkett – 140	Goslin – .6164
7.	Clarke – 122.84	Henderson – 126.14	Medwick – 134	Manush – .6818
8.	Manush – 117.74	Medwick – 125.35	Kelley – 134	O'Rourke – .7057
9.	Simmons – 117.31	Burkett – 125.18	O'Rourke – 134	Raines – .7263
10.	Raines – 115.71	Manush – 125.14	Simmons – 133	Kiner – .709
11.	Kiner – 113.49	Stargell – 124.31	Clarke – 133	Yastrzemski – .755
12.	Goslin – 113.10	Kelley – 119.22	Hafey – 133	Henderson – .7735
13.	Hafey – 109.89	Raines – 120.5	Yastrzemski – 130	Wheat – .88
14.	Brock – 109.22	B Williams – 113.99	Wheat – 129	B Williams – 1.001
15.	Medwick – 107.26	Yastrzemski–110.33	Goslin – 128	Simmons – 1.198
16.	Rice – 103.06	Rice – 110.23	Rice – 128	Medwick – 1.261
17.	Stargell – 96.95	Clarke – 105.50	Manush – 128	Hafey – 1.282
18.	B Williams – 96.18	Wheat – 104.86	Henderson – 127	Stargell – 2.066
19.	Yastrzemski – 93.41	O'Rourke – 104.09	Raines – 123	Rice – 2.124
20.	Wheat – 91.20	Brock – 102.57	Brock – 109	Brock – 2.273

	oWAR/162	HR/162	RBI/162
1.	T Williams – 10.10	Kiner – 43.13	T Williams – 146.6
2.	Kiner – 6.36	T Williams – 41.64	Simmons – 142.3
3.	Delahanty – 6.22	Stargell – 38.57	Delahanty – 131.8
4.	Henderson – 6.13	Rice – 30.42	Stargell – 125.0
5.	Stargell – 5.21	B Williams – 29.06	Medwick – 123.8
6.	Burkett – 5.14	Simmons – 23.9	Goslin – 123.0
7.	Raines – 5.10	Yastrzemski – 23.25	Kiner – 118.6
8.	Simmons – 4.86	Hafey – 23.19	Hafey – 117.8
9.	Kelley – 4.73	Goslin – 18.93	Rice – 115.6
10.	O'Rourke – 4.71	Medwick – 18.35	Kelley – 111.6
11.	Goslin – 4.69	Henderson – 17.31	Manush – 108.14
12.	Medwick – 4.58	Raines – 12.52	B Williams – 100.6
13.	B Williams – 4.54	Brock – 10.11	Yastrzemski – 99.99
14.	Clarke – 4.46	Manush – 10.06	O'Rourke – 99.56
15.	Hafey – 4.44	Wheat – 9.34	Wheat – 88.3
16.	Manush – 4.21	Delahanty – 9.08	Clarke – 76.9
17.	Yastrzemski – 4.02	Kelley – 6.08	Burkett – 76.2
18.	Wheat – 3.88	Burkett – 6.00	Raines – 72.2
19.	Rice – 3.64	O'Rourke – 5.11	Henderson – 65.0
20.	Brock – 3.26	Clarke – 5.07	Brock – 61.05

THE DEFENSIVE COMPARISONS

dWAR/162	FP/162 to League	RF/162 to League
1. Yastrzemski: + .0514	Raines - .988/.979	Delahanty: + 43.74
2. Simmons: - .0856	Simmons - .988/.968	Clarke: + 40.50
3. Henderson: - .1341	Yastrzemski - .982/.977	Kelley: + 11.34
4. Clarke: - .2045	Manush - .982/.967	Yastrzemski: + 8.10
5. Goslin: - .3587	Medwick - .980/.976	Burkett: 0
6. Medwick: - .4298	Rice - .980/.981	Wheat: - 1.62
7. Delahanty: - .4855	Henderson - .979/980	Goslin: - 6.48
8. Wheat: - .4882	T Williams - .974/.977	Manush: - 9.72
9. Raines: - .6334	Kiner - .973/.975	Simmons: - 12.96
10. Rice: - .6371	B Williams - .973/.976	Rice: - 16.20
11. Kelley: - .6917	Hafey - .972/.971	Stargell: - 17.82
12. Manush: - .7039	Wheat - .967/.963	Hafey: - 27.54
13. Brock: - .7327	Stargell - .961/.970	Raines: - 25.92
14. Hafey: - .7920	Goslin - .960/.966	Medwick: - 25.92
15. O'Rourke: - .8406	Brock - .958/.970	Kiner: - 32.40
16. Burkett: - .9838	Kelley - .955/.933	O'Rourke: - 35.64
17. T Williams: - 1.063	Clarke - .952/.945	Henderson: - 37.26
18. B Williams: - 1.228	Delahanty - .951/.927	Brock: - 37.26
19. Kiner: - 1.251	Burkett - .917/.934	B Williams: - 42.12
20. Stargell: - 1.583	O'Rourke - .892/.878	T Williams: - 48.60

OBSERVATIONS AND COMMENTARY

Noticeable moves from JAWS to SAWS:

Ralph Kiner goes from 14th to 4th
Billy Williams goes from 8th to 14th
Carl Yastrzemski goes from 3rd to 11th

The 60% cutoff is 5.90 and eliminates all but three. The cutoff using the second highest score of 3.89 only eliminates Jim Rice and Lou Brock. The median is 4.97 and eliminates Carl Yastrzemski.

1. Ted Williams – 1939-1960, WAR 1st, JAWS, 1st

Missing almost five seasons to the military left him with 12.5 effective seasons. Five more seasons in the middle of his career probably would not have changed his seasonal calculations but it would have answered all the "what if" questions about how many career statistics he could have accumulated. His seasonal oWAR is the only one in double digits besides Babe Ruth and his SAWS just barely misses the "10" mark. He is second only to Ruth in dominance ranking. Delahanty does top him in BA and season adjusted runs scored and Kiner bests him in season adjusted home runs but the rest of the categories provide him with blue ribbons. Yes, his defensive ability was terrible as noted by the seventeenth place for dWAR and his last place in range factor above/below league. Easy first ballot vote but only with 93.4%. It was well known he was not friendly with the press.

2. Rickey Henderson – 1979-2003, WAR 2nd, JAWS 2nd

Henderson is an example of quality and quantity equal to that of the superstars such as Williams, Hornsby, Wagner, Mays and Ruth. He played for 25 seasons and still kept a second place under SAWS as well as JAWS and WAR. He did it with only moderate power, which was seventeenth in home runs and nineteenth in runs batted in, and the lowest BA, .279, of all left fielders. He had a good eye at the plate and that produced an OBP of .401 from a decent twelfth place SO/BB ratio. Once he got on base it was "off to the races" as he stole 1406 for almost 82 per effective season. That led to the all-time career lead in runs scored of 2295 which put him fifth in season adjusted runs scored. He was seventh in runs created. 3055 hits, twelve league leadership in stolen bases, one MVP, ten All-Star games and third best in season adjusted dWAR even with a negative range factor compared to league. He registered 94.8% on his first ballot and it should have been higher.

3. Ed Delahanty – 1888-1903, WAR 4th, JAWS 4th

As mentioned earlier he actually tops Ted Williams in season adjusted runs scored and batting average which put him third in oWAR. That rank also came from being second in OBP and runs created, third in SLG, OPS and RBI, and fourth in SO/BB. He was also seventh in dWAR with a first-place range factor above league, so he was a complete player. He had eighteen league leaderships in the six main batting categories, which makes him eleventh in dominance and finished with a .300/.400/.500 slash line. After his premature death it took seven ballots ranging from 7.5% to 52% before the Old Timers Committee of 1945 adopted him. He was one of the best the OTC chose in its two-year existence.

4. Ralph Kiner – 1946-1955, WAR 16th, JAWS 14th

Kiner joins Jackie Robinson, Hank Greenberg, Addie Joss, Joe DiMaggio and several others as one of the poster boys for SAWS. Here he moves up from sixteenth in WAR and fourteenth in JAWS to his rightful position. Overall, he moved from 118th in WAR and 96th in JAWS to 51st in SAWS. His oWAR is second only to Williams but his dWAR is extremely weak in nineteenth place. His .279 BA is next to last. But, in the short span of ten years, he hit 369 home runs at the seasonally adjusted rate of 43.13, second only to Babe Ruth. Other category rankings include second in SLG and OPS, fourth in runs created and OPS+, sixth in OBP and seventh in runs batted in. He led the league seven consecutive times in homers. He collected six All-Star appointments and seven MVP considerations but no prize. Amazingly in his first year on the BBWAA ballot he received 1.1% of the vote. How unbelievable is that? It is a sorry indication that writers imposed more of a playing tenure for Hall status than the actual Hall of Fame did. Or maybe they just did not like his weak defensive ability. It was only after his fifteenth ballot did he amass 75.4% of the vote and just barely squeeze in.

5. <u>Al Simmons – 1924-1944, WAR 6th, JAWS 5th</u>

Al Simmons was a complete player. His adjusted oWAR was only eighth but he was frequently in the upper echelons of the comparative categories. Those rankings include second in runs batted in, third in SLG and runs created, fourth in BA and OPS, and sixth in OBP and season adjusted home runs. His dWAR was second and just a hair from positive. His fielding percentage was second and he was twenty points above the league. He appeared in three All-Star games after their inception in 1933 and three World Series where he batted .329. He led the league in BA twice and RBI once. He collected 2927 hits on his way to a .334 career BA. He also stole 176 bases. Yet it took him ten ballots to reach 75.4%. The writers were tough.

6. <u>Fred Clarke – 1894-1915, WAR 7th, JAWS 9th</u>

Fred Clarke was overshadowed and almost overlooked as a left fielder and a player. He competed with Delahanty for the first several years and then went to player-manager. There he managed Honus Wagner, recognized by many as the first superstar of the modern era beginning in 1901. Another more complete player presents himself, though. Although his oWAR was fourteenth due to his lack of power which was very prevalent in his era, he still rapped out 2678 hits. He was third in SO/BB ratio, but other categories were not as good. Although he was seventh in OBP he was eleventh in BA and OPS+. He fell to sixteenth in SLG and runs batted in. Then he slid a little more to seventeenth in OPS, runs scored and runs created. Finally, the skid stopped at twentieth in home runs. He stole 509 bases and had a good eye at the plate with .396 OBP. He was fourth in dWAR and second in range factor with 40 season adjusted plays more than league average. After seven ballots rising only to 24.9% the Old Timers Committee of 1945 made one of its more justifiable choices.

7. <u>Tim Raines – 1979-2002 (excluding 2000), WAR 5th, JAWS, 6th</u>

Until I developed SAWS and Raines got elected I would have passed on him quickly and the writers did for nine ballots. His oWAR was seventh primarily from his

OBP, runs scored, runs created and his fifth place SO/BB ratio. Of course, once he got on base he stole 808 bases, fifth all-time, at a successful rate of 84.7% which is thirteenth in the history books. He led the league four times in SB and one time each in BA and OBP. He was second in the Rookie of the Year balloting. He collected seven All-Star appointments and seven considerations for MVP but only came in fifth in one of them. His dWAR was ninth with a high fielding percentage but a negative range factor. He came in on his tenth ballot with 86% which is a little higher than I would have anticipated. Last ballot selections do lend themselves to some sympathy votes. I am still ambivalent about Raines. He was unassuming and did not set any records.

8. Goose Goslin – 1921-1938, WAR 8th, JAWS 7th

Goslin manages to stay above median without anything all that impressive. His oWAR drops to eleventh but his comparative statistics stay pretty much that or higher. He was sixth in runs created and SO/BB ratio, seventh in OPS, eighth in OBP, ninth in SLG, tenth in BA, and twelfth in runs scored. He was better at defense as he is fifth in dWAR but his fielding percentage was six points below league average and his range factor was negative. His best count was sixth in six MVP races, he got one All-Star appointment after 1933, and led the league in BA once. He appeared in five World Series and hit seven homers with nineteen runs batted in. After ten unsuccessful ballots with .8% to 13.5% of the vote the 1968 Veterans Committee shined a light on him. He is above median overall and appears to be a very good player, but some committee selections are suspect. Besides, the Hall of Fame is for players who are more than just "very good." Something great or famous might be nice too.

9. Jesse Burkett – 1890-1905, WAR 10th, JAWS 10th

A .338 BA with a .415 OBP and 2850 hits are hard to ignore no matter which era or who they come from. His nickname was the "Crab" and not because he ran sideways. True to his era he played "small ball" with no power but he was sixth in the room in oWAR. He was fourth in runs scored, fifth in SO/BB and sixth in OPS+. Then he was ninth in runs created and OPS. His power figures were low at fifteenth in SLG, eighteenth in HR and seventeenth in RBI. He led the league in BA three times, two of those times batting over .400 but the mid-1890s was notorious for high BAs after the pitcher's box/mound was moved back to 60'6". His fielding was terrible as he was sixteenth in dWAR and had a fielding percentage seventeen percentage points below league average and only matched league range factor. I would be crabby too with that. After six ballots with all of 1.7% of the votes the 1946 Old Timers Committee was up to it usual tricks and selected him. Anything from the 1946 committee should be scrutinized no matter what a calculated number says.

10. Joe "Ducky" Medwick – 1932-1948, WAR 13th, JAWS 12th

His oWAR comes in twelfth and he tends to dance up and down above and below the median in the traditional and adjusted statistics. He was fifth in runs batted in, sixth in BA, and seventh in OPS+ and SLG. Next came eighth in OPS and runs created. A slight jump takes us to tenth with home runs. Then he goes to fifteenth in runs scored and sixteenth in SO/BB. His dWAR is sixth despite a poor range factor of -26 and four points below league average in fielding percentage. He is much better known for other things. First, he is the last National League Triple Crown winner in 1937 which resulted in the one MVP he collected out of eight considerations. He was elected to the All-Star squads some ten times and has seven league leaderships. He is also known for a dispute about sliding into third base and getting spiked in the 1934 World Series. The Detroit fans did not take to his actions and he had to be removed from the game for it to continue. In two World Series he did bat .326. Slowly but surely, he climbed the ladder of the BBWAA ballot from .8% to 84.5% over eleven ballots. Let me think about this one.

11. Carl Yastrzemski – 1961-1983, WAR 3rd, JAWS 3rd

"Yaz" shows the flaw in a single, calculated number. If he had retired two years earlier, rather than stay on as a DH, he would have been sixth. If he had retired four years earlier, he would have been fourth. But he would not have played in 3308 games which puts him second behind Pete Rose. And he would probably not have achieved 3000 hits or even 400 home runs. His Triple Crown of 1967 was the last one for 45 years. That single year's WAR was 12.5 and the third best position player WAR in baseball history behind Ruth who hold the first two slots. He had sixteen league leaderships in the main batting categories. He had one MVP from fourteen considerations, eighteen All-Star selections, and seven Gold Gloves. He is the only left fielder with a positive dWAR and one of only four with a positive range factor. He was, of course, a first ballot selectee with 94.6%. He is not median player, he is upper echelon.

12. Joe Kelley – 1891-1908, WAR 15th, JAWS 15th

His oWAR is ninth and pretty much confirmed by the comparative statistics. Those statistics say he was second in SO/BB, fourth in OBP and sixth in runs scored. He was eighth in BA and OPS+ tenth in RBI. Those were followed by a twelfth place in runs created and thirteenth in SLG and OPS. Last was seventeenth in home runs. His dWAR is sixteenth but he was 22 points above league average in fielding. On top of that he did steal or advance 443 bases and led the league in that category once. He served as player-manager for the last few years of his career. In two ballots he rounded up all of .4% but was elected by the Veterans Committee of 1971. That speaks volumes to me because there is nothing unique or special about this player.

13. Willie Stargell – 1962-1982, WAR 12th, JAWS 11th

He may be better remembered as "Pops" the MVP of the 1979 "We Are Family" World Series. It was exciting to watch. The image is backed up by some comparative statistics of power. He is fifth in oWAR from being third with home runs and fourth with runs batted in. His seasonal adjusted home runs rank fourteenth among all Hall members. He is also fourth in SLG, fifth in OPS+ and sixth in OPS. The balance to this act comes from a terrible SO/BB ratio of eighteenth (2.066) and a dWAR of twentieth with a fielding percentage nine points below league average. He picked up one MVP, came in second twice and third once in eleven considerations. He led the league six times in batting categories and collected seven All-Star appointments. He was a first ballot choice with 82.4%. I can easily live with this one. Home runs and image control here.

14. Billy Williams – 1959-1976, WAR 9th, JAWS 8th

He comes in thirteenth in oWAR and second in OPS+. The rest of his offensive comparisons are fifth in home runs, tenth in SLG, twelfth in OPS and RBI, fourteenth in runs created and SO/BB, sixteenth in BA and OPB and eighteenth in runs scored. Defense was not a strong point as he came in eighteenth with a poor fielding percentage three points below league average and nineteenth place range factor of -42. He was Rookie of the Year and came in second twice in eight MVP ballots. He had three league leaderships, one each in BA, SLG and OPS. He garnered six All-Star appointments. He had 2711 hits but finished his career with 251 games at DH. In six BBWAA ballots he climbed from 23% to 85.7%. I am somewhat ambivalent about Williams.

15. Zack Wheat – 1909-1927, WAR 11th, JAWS 13th

He fills the left field gap between Fred Clarke and Goose Goslin so there is no one to truly compare him to in his era. His oWAR drops to eighteenth and his dWAR comes up to eighth which is an unusual direction for both for left fielders. Offensively his best rank was ninth in BA. Second best was thirteenth in SO/BB followed by fourteenth in OPB, SLG and OPS+. Fifteenth was the slot for OPS, home runs and runs batted in. Pulling up the rear was eighteenth in runs created and runs scored. The dWAR comparisons were median at 12th for fielding percentage and four points above league average and a range factor of negative 1.6. He came in third once for MVP in three counts. He led the league in BA and SLG once and he had 2884 hits. After sixteen ballots and rising to 23% he was selected by the 1959 Veterans Committee. I think he would clearly be in the Dodger Hall of Fame but not as clear for the baseball Hall of Fame.

16. Chick Hafey – 1924-1937, WAR 20th, JAWS 20th

He may have been elevated by SAWS, but he is still dead last in WAR and JAWS. The man only had 1466 hits playing only thirteen seasons. He came in all of fifth in four MVP votes. He led the league in BA and SLG once and got one All-Star selection. Remarkably in comparative statistics he is fifth in SLG and OPS, seventh in BA, and eighth in HR and RBI. His oWAR climbs a couple of spots to fourteenth. His dWAR came in at fifteenth with a poor range factor of -27. He had a bad eye at the plate with a 1.282 SO/BB ratio. He only batted .205 in four World Series. After twelve ballots with .4% to 10.8% the Veterans Committee of 1971 struck another low note, but he is not the worst. If you are only going to play the equivalent of seven years you need to do something everyone notices.

17. Jim O'Rourke – 1872-1893, 1904, WAR 14th, JAWS 19th

O'Rourke goes to tenth in oWAR with a mysteriously high OPS+ of 134 as the other comparative statistics don't seem to jive with that figure. You be the judge. He was third in runs scored, and eighth in SOBB. He was twelfth in BA and fourteenth in runs batted in. He was eighteenth in SLG and OBP. He wrapped it up with nineteenth in OPS and runs created. He did have 2639 hits and led the league in BA once and OBP twice. He is fifteenth in dWAR but he was fourteen points above league average in fielding but 35.64 plays less than league average in range factor. He was chosen by the Old Timers Committee of 1945. Bill Lamb in his Player Bio for the SABR BioProject has an excellent piece on O'Rourke which may help explain his election. Maybe the combination of executive/pioneer and player is what got the committee's attention.

18. Heinie Manush – 1923-1939, WAR 18th, JAWS 17th

Heinie was a journeyman for seventeen years with six teams. His oWAR is actually sixteenth as he appears to be more median than low in the comparisons. He was fifth in BA and seventh in SO/BB. He was eighth in runs scored and tenth in runs created and OPS. Next was eleventh in SLG and runs batted in followed by twelfth in OBP. He was fourteenth in home runs and seventeenth in OPS+. His dWAR was even better at twelfth sporting a good fielding percentage of .982 to the league's .967 while being eighth in range factor. His career BA was .330 which falls in at 31st all-time and he did win one batting championship. He ended his career with 2524 hits. He had one All-Star selection and scratched out a second and a third in five MVP votes. After six writers' ballots with votes ranging from .7 to 9.4% the 1964 Veterans Committee gave him his ticket to Cooperstown. Why I don't know because he sure is not a household name.

19. Jim Rice – 1974-1989, WAR 17th, JAWS 16th

Despite being fourth in season adjusted home runs, ninth in runs batted in and eighth in SLG Rice comes in nineteenth in oWAR. Being nineteenth in SO/BB ratio in the room and fourth all-time among all players in grounded into double plays (GDP) might have had something to do with that. In fact, all the retired players above him in GDP had at least 21 seasons and he did it in sixteen. Sixteenth in runs created, runs scored and OPS+ doesn't help his case. Neither does nineteenth in OBP. And he never led the league in walks or intentional walks as a true slugger would. His dWAR was close to median but his fielding percentage was one percentage point below league average and his range factor was -16. He did have eight league leaderships in batting categories and one MVP out of eight looks with two Silver Sluggers. He was second in the Rookie of the Year campaign. He was voted to ten All-Star games and batted .333 in one World Series but no home runs or runs batted in to his credit. He did have 530 games at DH to accumulate his 2452 hits. He labored through fifteen ballots and slipped in on the last one with 76.4% of the voted, some of which were surely the sympathy on the last vote syndrome. I would not have voted for him. He is what I consider a "near slugger."

20. Lou Brock – 1961-1979, WAR 19th, JAWS 18th

Brock takes home last place in offensive categories more than any other player (eight). And his defense is bad as well with a fielding percentage of .958 compared to a league number of .970 and a - 37 range factor. So how can he possibly be a Hall of Famer and one who was elected on the first ballot? He collected 3000 hits without the aid of the DH. He broke Ty Cobb's and Billy Hamilton's career stolen base record and set a new single season record. He batted .391 in three World Series and set the World Series stolen base record. He was a big name, big game player.

THE OTHERS

Manny Ramirez was suspended for drug use. Fuggedaboutit!!!

CENTERFIELDERS

THE SEASONS

	Actual	Total Effective	Effective in CF
1.	Ty Cobb – 24	17.8381	17.7476
2.	Willie Mays – 22	17.1971	16.6882
3.	Tris Speaker – 22	16.3484	16.2538
4.	Ken Griffey – 22	15.1763	12.5425
5.	Andre Dawson – 21	14.8903	6.1727
6.	Max Carey – 20	14.6447	14.6447
7.	Mickey Mantle – 18	13.1788	10.2045
8.	Duke Snider – 18	11.0206	9.1834
9.	Edd Rousch – 18	11.2263	11.1427
10.	Lloyd Waner – 18	10.6385	10.6255
11.	Hugh Duffy – 17	10.3676	10.1495
12.	Richie Ashburn – 15	12.6264	11.8724
13.	Billy Hamilton – 14	9.5089	9.5089
14.	Joe DiMaggio – 13	10.3667	10.3608
15.	Earl Averill – 13	9.5597	9.5597
16.	Larry Doby – 13	8.5077	7.807
17.	Kirby Puckett – 12	10.03	8.3985
18.	Earle Combs – 12	8.1529	8.1529
19.	Hack Wilson – 12	7.524	7.4938

THE RANKINGS

	SAWS	WAR	JAWS
1.	Willie Mays – 9.09	Mays – 156.4	Mays – 115
2.	Ty Cobb – 8.47	Cobb – 151	Cobb – 110
3.	Mickey Mantle – 8.37	Speaker – 134.1	Speaker – 98.2
4.	Tris Speaker – 8.20	Mantle – 110.3	Mantle – 87.6
5.	Joe DiMaggio – 7.53	Griffey – 83.8	Griffey – 68.9
6.	Billy Hamilton – 6.67	DiMaggio – 78.1	DiMaggio – 64.5
7.	Duke Snider – 6.029	Snider – 66.3	Snider – 58.1
8.	Larry Doby – 5.83	Dawson – 64.8	Ashburn – 53.9
9.	Ken Griffey – 5.52	Ashburn – 63.9	Dawson – 54.2
10.	Earle Combs – 5.21	Hamilton – 63.4	Hamilton – 53.0
11.	Hack Wilson – 5.17	Carey – 54.0	Doby – 44.6
12.	Kirby Puckett – 5.08	Puckett – 51.1	Puckett – 44.4
13.	Richie Ashburn – 5.06	Doby – 49.6	Carey – 43.5

14. Earl Averill – 5.02	Averill – 48.0	Averill – 42.7
15. Andre Dawson – 4.38	Rousch – 45.3	Combs – 38.4
16. Hugh Duffy – 4.16	Duffy – 43.1	Rousch – 38.4
17. Edd Rousch – 4.01	Combs – 42.5	Wilson – 37.3
18. Max Carey – 3.6	Wilson – 38.9	Duffy – 37.0
19. Lloyd Waner – 2.27	Waner – 24.1	Waner – 22.2

THE OFFENSIVE COMPARISONS

	BA	OBP	SLG	OPS
1.	Cobb - .366	Hamilton - .455	DiMaggio - .579	Mantle - .9773
2.	Speaker - .345	Cobb - .433	Mays - .5575	DiMaggio - .9771
3.	Hamilton - .344	Speaker - .428	Mantle - .5568	Cobb - .945
4.	Duffy - .326	Mantle - .421	Wilson - .545	Mays - .941
5.	Combs - .3247	DiMaggio - .398	Snider - .540	Wilson - .940
6.	DiMaggio - .3246	Combs - .397	Griffey - .538	Speaker - .9283
7.	Rousch - .323	Ashburn - .396	Averill - .534	Averill - .9283
8.	Puckett - .3181	Wilson - .395	Cobb - .512	Snider - .919
9.	Averill - .3178	Averill - .395	Speaker - .500	Griffey - .907
10.	Waner - .316	Duffy - .3859	Doby - .490	Hamilton - .888
11.	Wilson - .309	Doby - .3859	Dawson - .482	Doby - .876
12.	Ashburn - .308	Mays - .384	Puckett - .477	Combs - .859
13.	Mays - .302	Snider - .380	Combs - .462	Puckett - .8366
14.	Mantle - .298	Griffey - .370	Duffy - .451	Duffy - .8365
15.	Snider - .295	Rousch - .369	Rousch - .446	Rousch - .815
16.	Carey - .285	Carey - .361	Hamitlon - .432	Dawson - .806
17.	Griffey - .284	Puckett - .360	Waner - .393	Ashburn - .778
18.	Doby - .283	Waner - .353	Carey - .386	Waner - .7468
19.	Dawson - .279	Dawson - .323	Ashburn - .382	Carey - .7467

	Runs Scored/162	Runs Created/162	OPS+	SO/BB Ratio
1.	Hamilton – 178.46	Mantle – 154.34	Mantle – 172	Speaker - .2853
2.	Duffy – 149.89	DiMaggio – 151.35	Cobb – 168	Hamilton - .3045
3.	Combs – 145.47	Cobb – 141.10	Speaker – 157	Duffy - .4036
4.	DiMaggio – 134.08	Averill – 138.39	Mays – 156	Waner - .4119
5.	Averill – 128.04	Mays – 137.7	DiMaggio – 155	Combs - .4149
6.	Mantle – 127.17	Wilson – 136.9	Wilson – 144	DiMaggio - .4671
7.	Cobb – 125.80	Snider – 134.02	Hamiltion – 142	Ashburn - .4766
8.	Mays – 119.91	Speaker – 131.63	Snider – 140	Rousch - .5372

9. Wilson – 117.49	Griffey – 131.39	Doby – 136	Cobb - .5452
10. Speaker – 115.12	Hamilton – 128.83	Griffey – 136	Carey - .6683
11. Snider – 114.24	Combs – 128.05	Averill – 133	Averill - .6693
12. Doby – 112.93	Puckett – 119.74	Rousch – 126	Mantle - .9867
13. Waner – 112.89	Doby – 119.52	Combs – 125	Mays – 1.0423
14. Griffey – 109.51	Duffy – 119.31	Puckett – 124	Wilson – 1.1484
15. Puckett – 106.78	Ashburn – 105.65	Duffy – 123	Doby – 1.1607
16. Carey – 105.50	Rousch – 105.46	Dawson – 119	Snider – 1.2739
17. Ashburn – 104.70	Dawson – 102.5	Ashburn – 111	Griffey – 1.3559
18. Rousch – 97.90	Waner – 102.08	Carey – 108	Puckett – 2.144
19. Dawson – 92.71	Carey – 91.77	Waner – 99	Dawson – 2.562

oWAR /162	HR/162	RBI/162
1. Mantle – 8.83	Griffey – 41.51	DiMaggio – 148.26
2. Cobb – 8.48	Mantle – 40.67	Wilson – 141.28
3. Mays – 7.95	Mays – 38.38	Duffy – 125.58
4. Speaker – 7.60	Snider – 36.93	Averill – 121.76
5. DiMaggio – 7.08	DiMaggio – 34.82	Griffey – 120.98
6. Hamilton – 6.50	Wilson – 32.43	Snider – 120.96
7. Snider – 6.42	Doby – 29.67	Mantle – 114.5
8. Wilson – 5.68	Dawson – 29.58	Doby – 114.11
9. Doby – 5.65	Averill – 24.90	Mays – 110.66
10. Griffey – 5.57	Puckett – 20.64	Cobb – 108.36
11. Averill – 5.35	Duffy – 10.22	Dawson – 107.43
12. Puckett – 5.28	Ashburn – 8.63	Puckett – 102.13
13. Combs – 5.14	Speaker – 7.16	Speaker – 93.65
14. Ashburn – 4.59	Combs – 7.11	Rousch – 87.38
15. Rousch – 4.12	Cobb – 6.56	Hamilton – 78.03
16. Dawson – 3.74	Rousch – 6.06	Combs – 77.64
17. Duffy – 3.68	Carey – 4.78	Waner – 56.21
18. Carey – 3.11	Hamilton – 4.21	Carey – 54.75
19. Waner – 2.17	Waner – 2.54	Ashburn – 46.41

THE DEFENSIVE COMPARISONS

dWAR/162	FP/162 to League	RF/162 to League
1. Mays: + 1.06	Puckett - .990/.986	Speaker: + 90.72
2. Ashburn + .428	Griffey - .986/.987	Carey: + 81.0
3. DiMaggio: + .309	Doby - .986/.982	Waner: + 77.56

4. Speaker: + .153	Snider - .985/.978	Puckett: + 63.18
5. Griffey: + .145	Dawson - .984/.984	Ashburn: + 56.70
6. Carey: - .007	Ashburn - .983/.982	DiMaggio: + 53.46
7. Doby: - .012	Waner - .983/.976	Doby: + 46.98
8. Puckett: - .030	Mantle - .982/.980	Rousch: + 45.36
9. Dawson: - .108	Mays - .981/.981	Combs: + 42.12
10. Waner: - .197	DiMaggio - .978/.974	Hamilton: + 35.64
11. Duffy: - .241	Combs - .974/.967	Cobb: + 32.40
12. Combs: - .331	Rousch - .971/.968	Averill: + 27.54
13. Rousch: - .535	Speaker - .970/.960	Dawson: + 27.54
14. Snider: - .535	Averill - .970/.968	Mays: + 19.44
15. Hamilton: - .547	Carey - .966/.963	Snider: + 9.72
16. Averill: - .554	Wilson - .965/.971	Duffy: + 9.72
17. Cobb: - .605	Cobb - .961/.960	Wilson: - 12.96
18. Mantle: - .728	Duffy - .943/.923	Griffey: - 16.2
19. Wilson: - .955	Hamilton - .926/.928	Mantle: - 38.88

OBSERVATIONS AND COMMENTARY

Noticeable moves from JAWS to SAWS:

Billy Hamilton moves from 10th to 6th
Larry Doby moves from 11th to 8th
Andre Dawson goes from 9th to 15th
Earl Combs goes from 15th to 10th
Hack Wilson goes from 17th to 11th
Ken Griffey goes from 5th to 9th

The 60% cutoff is 5.45. The median is Earle Combs at 5.21.

1. Willie Mays – 1951-1973, WAR 1st, JAWS, 1st

   There is so much you can say about Willie Mays but little needs to be said. And he missed two seasons that would have moved his WAR and JAWS up and it is highly doubtful that it would affect his SAWS. He may not come in first in any of the offensive comparison categories, but he was so well rounded that it did not matter. He did come in first in dWAR. Astoundingly he only got 94.7% of the BBWAA vote. Even in 1979 the writers should have been smart enough to know greatness when they saw it. Apparently not.

2. Ty Cobb – 1905-1928, WAR 2nd, JAWS 2nd

Cobb is another player that needs no introduction. Many of his records stood for over a half century before others like Brock, Rose and Henderson broke them. No one has come close to his .366 BA, though. People who say he could not hit for power should realize he was so capable with a bat that he chose not to swing for the fences. He proved his point on May 5 and 6, 1925 hitting 5 home runs. He also won a Triple Crown and captured 42 league leaderships in six batting categories making him the fifth most dominant player in the history of the game. He was an "Immortal" with 98.2% of the vote.

3. Mickey Mantle – 1951-1968, WAR 4th, JAWS 4th

Blessed with not only an alliterative name one can only imagine what he could have done with a healthy pair of legs. Many now say he played a full career with a torn ACL in his knee. He owns the highest oWAR in centerfield and is second highest in season adjusted home runs. He took first place in the offensive comparison categories of OPS, OPS+ and runs created. A Triple Crown was his to boast about. So were three MVPs and three more in second place. Seventeen All-Star selections in eighteen years can be tacked on to his list. Cumulative World Series records flow into his portfolio. How about nineteen league leaderships which is fourteenth in dominance? His dWAR was pretty bad, though, especially his range factor which was negative 39. He only had 2415 hits and let his BA slip below .300. He only got 88.2% of the first ballot vote. Amazing it was that low.

4. Tris Speaker – 1907-1928, WAR 3rd, JAWS 3rd

A very complete and consistent player. He is fourth in oWAR and dWAR. He comes in second to Cobb with a .345 BA. He is third in OBP and OPS+. He is first in SO/BB ratio. He has above a .300/.400/.500 slash line. He even stole 436 bases. He had nine league leaderships and one MVP stymied by that American League rule of one only which existed in the 1920s. He batted .306 in three World Series. He is the all-time leader in doubles with 792. The "Grey Eagle" excelled in the outfield as he has a first place + 90.72 seasonal adjusted range factor and a full ten-point advantage on the league fielding percentage. Another strange vote with him only receiving 82.1% on the second 1937 ballot. Ruth, Cobb and Wagner were a hard act to follow.

5. Joe DiMaggio – 1936-1951, WAR 6th, JAWS, 6th

He only had thirteen seasons due to three prime years spent in the military, so WAR and JAWS relegate him to a lower position than Ken Griffey which is wrong. Since Joe played 10.3667 effective years and Junior played 15.1763, Joe only needed 68% of the playing time to acquire 93% of the WAR Junior had. Or Junior took 46.4% more time to accumulate 7.3% more WAR than Joe. Here are all the centerfielder comparisons in rank for the two.

BA – Joe DiMaggio (JD) is 6th, Ken Griffey (KG) is 17th

OBP – JD is 5th, KG is 14th

SLG – JD is 1st, KG is 6th

OPS – JD is 2nd, KG is 9th

OPS+ – JD is 6th, KG is 10th

SO/BB – JD is 6th, KG is 17th

Season Adjusted Runs Batted In – JD is 1st, KG is 5th

Season Adjusted Runs Scored – JD is 4th, KG is 14th

Season Adjusted Runs Created – JD is 2nd, KG is 9th

Season Adjusted oWAR – JD is 5th, KG is 10th

Season Adjusted dWAR – JD is 3rd, KG is 5th

Season Adjusted Home Runs – KG is 1st, JD is 6th

Joe also had three MVPs and two second place results in twelve votes. He was selected for the All-Star game in all thirteen of his playing seasons. He had eight league leaderships. He had a 56-game hitting streak that captured the attention of the country. Not only was he fifth in oWAR he was third in dWAR so I wonder how many Silver Sluggers and Gold Gloves he would have won. Not counting a vote during his playing career, it still took three ballots to get Joe enshrined and with only 88% of the vote.

6. Billy Hamilton – 1888-1901, WAR 10th, JAWS 10th

"Sliding Billy" had definite reasons to brag. He was sixth in season adjusted oWAR in a room full of superstars. He batted .344 which is third in this impressive room. He was first in OBP and runs scored and his eye at the plate came in second in SO/BB. Only in the power categories of HR, RBI and SLG did he post lower than tenth. He got on base and stole or advanced some 914 times which some consider to be the career record Lou Brock broke. He had nine league leaderships in batting and five more each in stolen bases and base on balls. His dWAR sinks to fifteenth as he had a poor fielding percentage of two points below league average and a positive (+35) range factor above league average. He got one look from the 1936 Veterans Committee who showered him with all of 2.4% of the vote. The 1961 Veterans Committee got it right.

7. Duke Snider – 1947-1964, WAR 7th, JAWS 7th

Another very consistent player in that he is seventh in season adjusted oWAR and dWAR. He was also seventh in WAR and JAWS. Offensively his strong points are home runs, runs batted in and SLG. Take a very close look at all the following offensive comparisons and you will see that he beats Griffey in all categories except for home runs and runs batted in. Fifteenth in BA and thirteenth in OBP. Eighth in OPS and OPS+. Seventh in runs created and eleventh in runs scored. Sixteenth in SO/BB and seventh in oWAR. And he lost the RBI contest by .02 RBI per effective season. He got eight All-Star appointments and a first, second, third and fourth place in eight MVP ballots. He also led the league in batting categories seven times. In dWAR he loses to Griffey, but his FP is seven percentage points better than the league while Griffey's is only four. Then look at range factor. Snider had a positive one whereas Griffey was one of the only two centerfielders with a negative range factor. I think it borders on criminal that it took eleven ballots to elect Snider.

8. Larry Doby – 1947-1959, WAR 13th, JAWS 11th

Almost forgotten as the first to break the color barrier in the American League, he slips slightly in oWAR to ninth and struggles to maintain his comparisons to median. He rates seventh in home runs and eighth in runs batted in. He is ninth in OPS+ and tenth in SLG. He comes in eleventh in OBP and OPS. His runs scored are twelfth and his runs created are thirteenth. He slips to fifteenth in SO/BB ratio and even more with his BA which comes in seventh. His dWAR is seventh with a fielding percentage four points higher than the league and a strong positive range factor of 47. He picked up seven All-Star appointments and had six league leaderships in batting categories. He placed second in four MVP tallies. Three BBWAA votes netted him a high of 3.4% but the 1998 Veterans Committee saw it differently. There are simply not enough reasons to have ignored him for so long.

9. Ken Griffey – 1989-2010, WAR 5th, JAWS 5th

Placing Ken Griffey as the closest thing to 100% for the Hall of Fame is an indication of how poor the BBWAA voters perform their job. His full record comes nowhere close to comparing to seven of the above eight players. He had a great first half of a career, but Jackie Robinson had a great second half of a career and got nowhere near the respect. It is almost like two different players played Griffey's career. He is tenth in oWAR and in six of the offensive comparison categories he is below median. He only had six league leaderships and everybody above him had that or more. Nineteen players had more than one seasonally adjusted league leadership and he had .395 so he was nowhere near dominant. He was only third in the Rookie of the Year voting. He only had one MVP and thirteen All-Star selections in 22 seasons. DiMaggio had three MVPs and thirteen selections to the All-Star squads in thirteen years. He won nine Gold Gloves, but finished with a negative range factor and a fielding percentage one point below league average. That helps the suggestion that changes need to be made to that selection process. (And I understand that is happening). He did collect 2781 hits but 2781 is not 3000. But 630 homers are an automatic selection? Only three voters had the mettle to say, "No."

10. Earle Combs – 1924-1935, WAR 17th, JAWS 15th

SAWS tilts the windmill in Combs's favor from seventeenth in WAR and fifteenth in JAWS as he only played twelve years. His oWAR is thirteenth and he has a mixed bag of rankings. He is third in runs scored, fifth in BA and SO/BB, and sixth in OPB. He is ninth in OPS+ and twelfth in OPS. He is eleventh in runs created and thirteenth in SLG. He is fourteenth in home runs and sixteenth in runs batted in. He had no league leaderships unless you go to the more peripheral categories of hits and triples. He only placed sixth in two MVP votes. His dWAR was twelfth and he showed well in range factor (+42) but not fielding percentage as he was three points under league average. He watched fourteen ballots provide him with up to 16% of the vote before the 1970 Veterans Committee brought him in. There is not enough to warrant this selection. Sometimes I think some players are brought in by association with other great players. Not in my Hall of Fame.

11. Hack Wilson – 1923-1924, WAR 18th, JAWS 17th

Again, we have a twelve-season player who scored poorly in WAR and JAWS. This one had some pop in his bat, though. His oWAR is eighth and he was second in RBI, fourth in SLG, fifth in OPS, and sixth in home runs, OPS and runs created so he had offensive capabilities. He had eight league leaderships, not counting the five in strikeouts, and still has the major league RBI season record of 191. His dWAR is pitiful at nineteenth. He was six percentage points below league in fielding percentage and negative in his season adjusted range factor. He was basically a 5'6", 190 lb. drunk who gave the ball a ride. After sixteen ballots he rose from .4 to 38.3% but the 1979 Veterans Committee liked him. I think he is more anecdotal than anything great or famous.

12. Kirby Puckett – 1984-1995, WAR 12th, JAWS 12th

This is the third player in a row with a twelve-year career. His unfortunately ended with an eye malady. It is, though, hard to ignore a recent .318 BA and someone who led the league in hits four times. Other than that, he had one league leadership in RBI. He hangs on to twelfth for his oWAR but he is below median in many categories. His SO/BB ratio is terrible and over two. There are no single digits in his offensive rankings. He is tenth in home runs and twelfth in RBI, runs created and SLG. He is thirteenth in OPS, fourteenth in OPS+ and fifteenth in runs created. Bringing up the rear is OBP at seventeen. His dWAR was better at eighth with a good fielding percentage and strong range factor. He collected ten All-Star positions and six Gold Gloves and Silver Sluggers. He placed second once in nine MVP votes and batted .308 in two World Series. He vaulted into the Hall on the first ballot with 82.1%. He wasn't *that* good. Maybe at a later ballot but I am not necessarily one who thinks players get better as time goes by. If they are not good the first time up, they rarely improve.

13. Richie Ashburn – 1948-1962, WAR 9th, JAWS 8th

SAWS hurts him but he played fifteen years so it isn't a long career with the mistake of hanging on too long. It seems to be quality. His oWAR slips to fourteenth as he had little power at the plate. His comparison rankings are low as well. He starts with a seven ranking for OBP and SO/BB ratio, but it is downhill from there. Twelfth in BA and home runs coupled with fifteenth in runs created are only precursors to seventeenth in OPS, OPS+ and runs scored. Last is SLG and runs batted in at nineteenth. He led the league a total of six times, four in OBP, not counting the four times he led in BB. His dWAR shines at second in the room with a good fielding percentage and a very good range factor. He had five All-Star selections and came in seventh once in eight MVP counts. He was pretty much the forgotten man in the Mays-Mantle-Snider argument of the 1950s. He labored through fifteen ballots scratching and clawing up to 35.4% but had to wait for the 1995 Veterans Committee to praise him. He is just not there in my book.

14. Earl Averill – 1929-1941, WAR 14th, JAWS 14th

Another short career, this one lasting thirteen seasons, but it is not affected by SAWS. Averill maintains this same slot in WAR and JAWS. His oWAR says eleventh but the comparative statistics say higher. He was fourth in runs created and RBI, fifth in runs scored, seventh in SLG and OPS, and ninth in HR. He also had a decent SO/BB ratio. He had no league leaderships except once each in hits and triples, but he collected six All-Star appointments after 1933. His best MVP vote was third in seven tallies. His dWAR was poor at sixteenth but his fielding percentage and range factor are not that bad. He is somewhat of a mystery but not famous or great according to the writers who adorned him with a maximum of 5.3% of the votes in seven looks. The 1975 Veterans Committee entered the fracas to keep him immortal. I think it is becoming self-explanatory when a 1970s committee is involved.

15. Andre Dawson – 1976-1996, WAR 8th, JAWS 9th

If anyone hung on too long it is Andre Dawson. His last four years netted him about 300 games and a negative 2.3 WAR. SAWS will not be kind to him. He takes a hard fall from WAR and JAWS, but I intend to look at a player's full career, not pick and choose only that which looks good. His oWAR goes down even one more step to sixteenth. His best performances were eighth in HR and eleventh in RBI. He was dead last in BA, OPB, runs scored and SO/BB ratio and the only season adjusted number of that quartet is runs scored. The rest are traditional calculations. He was ninth in dWAR matching the league fielding percentage and thirteenth in range factor. He collected six Gold Gloves, four Silver Sluggers, two league leaderships (HR and RBI), Rookie of the Year Award, eight All-Star positions and one MVP and two seconds out of nine looks. All of that sounds like a lot until you realize he played 21 years. He snuck in on his ninth ballot with 77.8%. I would have made sure the door was locked.

16. Hugh Duffy – 1888-1901, 1904-1906, WAR 16th, JAWS 18th

His best statistic is the .440 he batted in 1894. But some of that bat is tempered with the fact that 1894 was the second year the pitcher's box of 55.5 feet was moved to a pitcher's mound at 60.5 feet. Batters had the advantage for two to three years. His oWAR stays close at seventeenth thanks to his eleventh position in home runs, his third position in RBI and his second position in runs scored. His BA in fourth place does not hurt but he can be weak elsewhere. Check out runs created, SLG and OPS where he came in fourteenth. He was fifteenth in OPS+. He did lead the league six times including twice in both home runs and batting average. His dWAR is better at eleventh with an excellent fielding percentage which was twenty points above league average and a positive range factor. Six writers' ballots pushed him up to the 33% vote level and the 1945 Old Timers Committee pulled him in. It was a questionable choice.

17. Edd Rousch – 1913-1931, WAR 15th, JAWS 16th

Rousch had a seventh place BA with .323 but not much else anywhere near the median, but not necessarily the bottom. Hence, his oWAR climbs to fifteenth. But note that he was fourteenth in runs batted in. And he was fifteenth in OBP, SLG, OPS and sixteenth in home runs and runs created. Dropping close to last he was eighteenth in runs scored. His dWAR is thirteenth thanks to a good fielding percentage and a positive range factor. He did win four league leaderships but two were for BA while one each was for SLG and OPS. In two MVP votes he came in tenth. He holds the record for nineteen ballots without being elected. His nineteenth ballot showed 54.3% and the Veterans Committee of 1962 led him down the garden path. I cannot understand the last BBWAA vote much less the enshrinement.

18. Max Carey – 1910-1929, WAR 11th, JAWS 13th

If at first you see 2665 hits and 738 stolen bases from ten league leading years of stolen bases you begin to think something is wrong with the rankings. Then you analyze the rankings and you see Carey is in a race to the bottom with Waner. He keeps the eighteen slot for oWAR. He was last in two offensive categories and next to last in four more. He was above sixteenth in one category, SO/BB. His dWAR comes in very high at sixth as he had a superb range factor of +81. He came in eleventh in three MVP votes. On fourteen ballots he went from .4% to 51.1% and again a Veterans Committee, this time in 1961, threw him the life line. Please read the last sentence of the previous commentary.

19. Lloyd Waner – 1927-1945, WAR 19th, JAWS 19th.

Waner is in a race to the bottom of the rankings of all position players. He comes in 156th in a 157-man race. He is last in this room and in WAR and JAWS. His dWAR shines a small ray of light at tenth thanks to a good fielding percentage and range factor above league average. He had one All-Star game after 1933 and placed fifth in one of five MVP ballots. He did have 2459 hits with a .316 BA. He had no league leaderships except one in hits. He climbed to 23.4% in ten ballots before the 1967 Veterans Committee anointed him. His brother Paul Waner had been inducted in 1952 so I suppose this committee thought the Hall of Fame was like Little League tryouts: if you take one brother you must take both.

THE OTHERS

Even though it is way too early in his career to be making projections, Mike Trout has a current (April 15, 2018) SAWS of 10.10!

RIGHTFIELDERS

THE SEASONS

	Actual	Total Effective	Effective at RF
1.	Hank Aaron – 23	19.1674	12.9479
2.	Babe Ruth – 22	13.9623	12.9746
3.	Stan Musial – 22	16.7048	10.8196
4.	Mel Ott – 22	15.4705	13.9177
5.	Al Kaline – 22	15.9204	11.5642
6.	Dave Winfield – 22	17.3361	10.9465
7.	Frank Robinson – 21	16.3416	7.4305
8.	Reggie Jackson – 21	16.0665	11.0592
9.	Paul Waner – 20	14.0905	13.7003
10.	Tony Gwynn – 20	13.7259	12.5388
11.	Sam Rice – 20	13.4973	9.0252
12.	Sam Crawford – 19	14.7483	13.8429
13.	Enos Slaughter – 19	12.0217	12.0217
14.	Willie Keeler – 19	12.4834	12.0549
15.	Roberto Clemente – 18	14.0702	13.6628
16.	KiKi Cuyler – 18	10.8395	10.8395
17.	Harry Heilmann – 17	12.3697	9.6111
18.	Harry Hooper – 17	13.7778	13.7764
19.	Chuck Klein – 17	9.4979	9.4966
20.	King Kelly – 16	8.8889	4.454
21.	Vladimir Guerrero – 16	12.5793	9.4435
22.	Sam Thompson – 15	8.4314	8.4266
23.	Elmer Flick – 13	8.8992	8.8038
24.	Tommy McCarthy – 13	7.7449	7.1920
25.	Ross Youngs – 10	7.2798	7.2380

THE RANKINGS

	SAWS	WAR	JAWS
1.	Babe Ruth – 11.61	Ruth – 162.1#	Ruth – 123.4
2.	Stan Musial – 7.64	Aaron – 143	Aaron – 101.7
3.	Hank Aaron – 7.46	Musial – 128.2	Musial – 96.2
4.	Mel Ott – 6.97	Ott – 107.8	Ott – 80.3
5.	Roberto Clemente – 6.72	FRobinson – 107.3	FRobinson – 80.1
6.	Frank Robinson – 6.57	Clemente – 94.5	Clemente – 74.3
7.	Elmer Flick – 5.98	Kaline – 92.8	Kaline – 70.8

8. Harry Heilmann – 5.84	Crawford – 75.2	RJackson – 60.4
9. Al Kaline – 5.83	RJackson – 74	Heilmann – 59.7
10. Sam Thompson – 5.27	Waner – 72.8	Waner – 57.5
11. Paul Waner – 5.17	Heilmann – 72.2	Crawford – 57.5
12. Sam Crawford – 5.10	Gwynn – 69.2	Gwynn – 55.2
13. Tony Gwynn – 5.04	Winfield – 64.2	Winfield – 51.1
14. King Kelly – 4.93	Guerrero – 59.4	Guerrero – 50.3
15. Vladimir Guerrero – 4.72	Slaughter – 55.3	Flick – 47.3
16. Reggie Jackson – 4.606	Keeler – 54.1	Slaughter – 45.3
17. Enos Slaughter – 4.60	Hooper – 53.4	Keeler – 45.2
18. Chuck Klein – 4.59	Flick – 53.2	Rice – 41.7
19. Ross Youngs – 4.42	Rice – 52.7	Hooper – 41.7
20. Willie Keeler – 4.37	Cuyler – 46.7	Cuyler – 40.8
21. KiKi Cuyler – 4.31	Thompson – 44.4	Klein – 40.1
22. Sam Rice – 3.90	Kelly – 44.3	Thompson – 38.7
23. Harry Hooper – 3.88	Klein – 43.6	Kelly – 37.7
24. Dave Winfield – 3.70	Youngs – 32.2	Youngs – 31.3
25. Tommy McCarthy – 2.09	McCarthy – 16.2	McCarthy – 17.6

Babe Ruth also has a pitching WAR of 20.4. Only the position player WAR will be used. No other player even scores in double digits for SAWS. If you add in the pitching WAR his total SAWS would be 13.29!

THE OFFENSIVE COMPARISONS

	BA	OPB	SLG	OPS
1.	Ruth - .3421	Ruth - .474	Ruth - .690	Ruth – 1.164
2.	Heilmann - .3416	Musial - .417	Musial - .559	Musial - .976
3.	Keeler - .341	Ott - .414	Aaron - .555	Ott - .947
4.	Gwynn - .338	Heilmann - .410	Guerrero - .553	Guerrero - .931
5.	Waner - .333	Waner - .404	Klein - .543	Heilmann - .930
6.	Thompson - .3314	Youngs - .399	Robinson - .537	Aaron - .928
7.	Musial - .3308	Cuyler - .396	Ott - .533	Robinson - .926
8.	Rice - .3223	Robinson - .3890	Heilmann - .520	Klein - .922
9.	Youngs - .3222	Flick - .3890	Thompson - .505	Thompson - .890
10.	Cuyler - .321	Gwynn - .3882	Jackson - .490	Waner - .878
11.	Klein - .320	Keeler - .3878	Kaline - .480	Cuyler - .860
12.	Guerrero - .318	Thompson - .384	Clemente - .4751	Kaline - .855
13.	Clemente - .317	Slaughter - .382	Winfield - .4745	Gwynn - .847

14.	Flick - .313	Klein - .3788	Cuyler - .474	Jackson - .846
15.	Crawford - .309	Guerrero - .3786	Waner - .473	Youngs - .839
16.	Kelly - .308	Kaline - .376	Gwynn - .459	Slaughter - .8345
17.	Aaron - .305	Aaron - .3739	Slaughter - .453	Clemente - .8344
18.	Ott - .304	Rice - .3739	Crawford - .452	Flick - .8343
19.	Slaughter - .300	Hooper - .3679	Flick - .445	Winfield - .827
20.	Kaline - .297	Kelly - .3677	Youngs - .441	Crawford - .814
21.	Robinson - .294	McCarthy - .364	Kelly - .438	Kelly - .806
22.	McCarthy - .292	Crawford - .362	Rice - .427	Keeler - .802
23.	Winfield - .283	Clemente - .359	Keeler - .415	Rice - .801
24.	Hooper - .281	Jackson - .356	Hooper - .387	Hooper - .755
25.	Jackson - .262	Winfield - .353	McCarthy - .375	McCarthy - .740

	Runs Scored/162	Runs Created/162	OPS+	SO/BB Ratio
1.	Ruth – 155.71	Ruth – 194.66	Ruth – 206	Keeler - .2595
2.	Kelly – 152.66	Musial – 153.37	Musial – 159	Waner - .3446
3.	Thompson – 149.66	Klein – 143.61	Aaron – 155	McCarthy - .3517
4.	Keeler – 138.81	Thompson – 138.06	Ott – 155	Rice - .3884
5.	McCarthy – 137.64	Ott – 134.84	Robinson – 154	Musial - .4353
6.	Klein – 122.97	Heilmann – 134.44	Flick – 149	Hooper - .5114
7.	Cuyler – 122.39	Aaron – 133.14	Heilmann – 148	Thompson - .5188
8.	Ott – 120.16	Guerrero – 129.26	Thompson – 147	Ott - .5246
9.	Musial – 116.67	Waner – 128.95	Crawford – 144	Slaughter - .5285
10.	Waner – 115.47	Robinson – 124.10	Guerrero – 140	Gwynn - .5494
11.	Aaron – 113.42	Cuyler – 120.12	Kelly – 139	Heilmann - .6425
12.	Rice – 112.17	Gwynn – 119.19	Jackson – 139	Ruth - .6450
13.	Robinson – 111.92	Kaline – 116.33	Klein – 137	Youngs - .7091
14.	Youngs – 111.54	Slaughter – 114.21	Waner – 134	Kelly - .7614
15.	Flick – 106.75	Keeler – 111.28	Kaline – 134	Crawford - .7632
16.	Guerrero – 105.57	Clemente – 110.73	Gwynn – 132	Kaline - .7987
17.	Heilmann – 104.37	Jackson – 110.23	Clemente – 130	Klein - .8669
18.	Slaughter – 103.73	Youngs – 109.21	Youngs – 130	Flick - .9497
19.	Hooper – 103.72	Rice – 108.47	Winfield – 130	Cuyler - .9645
20.	Kaline – 101.88	Kelly – 107.89	Keeler – 127	Aaron - .9722
21.	Gwynn – 100.76	Flick – 106.98	Cuyler – 125	Robinson – 1.077
22.	Clemente – 100.64	Crawford – 106.22	Slaughter – 124	Winfield – 1.3865
23.	Jackson – 96.54	Winfield – 104.58	Hooper – 114	Guerrero – 1.3365
24.	Winfield – 96.27	McCarthy – 91.42	Rice – 112	Jackson – 1.8887
25.	Crawford – 94.32	Hooper – 89.13	McCarthy – 102	Clemente – 1.9807

	oWAR/162	HR/162	RBI/162
1.	Ruth – 11.05	Ruth – 51.14	Ruth – 158.57
2.	Musial – 7.47	Aaron – 39.39	Thompson – 154.78
3.	Aaron – 6.91	Robinson – 35.86	Klein – 126.45
4.	Ott – 6.70	Guerrero – 35.69	Heilmann – 124.5
5.	Robinson – 6.55	Jackson – 35.04	Ott – 120.23
6.	Heilmann – 6.22	Ott – 33.03	Aaron – 119.84
7.	Flick – 5.71	Klein – 31.59	Guerrero – 118.93
8.	Kelly – 5.61	Musial – 28.43	Musial – 116.79
9.	Crawford – 5.44	Winfield – 26.82	Robinson – 110.88
10.	Thompson – 5.35	Kaline – 25.06	Slaughter – 108.47
11.	Waner – 5.06	Clemente – 17.06	Kelly – 106.89
12.	Klein – 5.0537	Thompson – 14.94	Jackson – 105.93
13.	Clemente – 5.0532	Heilmann – 14.79	Winfield – 105.73
14.	Kaline – 4.92	Slaughter – 14.06	Crawford – 103.61
15.	Gwynn – 4.90	Cuyler – 11.81	Kaline – 99.37
16.	Jackson – 4.81	Gwynn – 9.84	Cuyler – 98.25
17.	Guerrero – 4.70	Waner – 8.02	McCarthy – 94.51
18.	Slaughter – 4.50	Kelley – 7.77	Waner – 92.90
19.	Keeler – 4.28	Crawford – 6.58	Clemente – 92.75
20.	Winfield – 4.27	Youngs – 5.77	Flick – 84.95
21.	Youngs – 4.26	McCarthy – 5.68	Gwynn – 82.91
22.	Cuyler – 4.25	Hooper – 5.44	Youngs – 81.32
23.	Rice – 3.39	Flick – 5.39	Rice – 79.79
24.	Hooper – 3.29	Keeler – 2.66	Keeler – 65.41
25.	McCarthy – 2.09	Rice – 2.58	Hooper – 59.23

THE DEFENSIVE COMPARISONS

	dWAR	FP/162 to League	RF/162 to League
1.	Clemente: + .8671	Gwynn - .987/.978	Clemente: + 27.54
2.	Kaline: + .1759	Robinson - .986/.976	Kaline: + 24.30
3.	Ruth: - .1674	Musial - .985/.973	Aaron: + 17.82
4.	Aaron: - .240	Kaline - .984/.978	Jackson: - 3.24
5.	Hooper: - .3194	Winfield - .984/.977	Winfield: - 3.24
6.	Ott: - .3878	Rice - .981/.978	Cuyler: - 6.48
7.	Gwynn: - .4808	Slaughter - .980/.978	Guerrero: - 14.58
8.	Kelly: - .4950	Aaron - .980/.976	McCarthy: - 16.20
9.	Cuyler: - .5074	Ott - .979/.970	Robinson: - 19.44

10. Musial: - .5507	Cuyler - .976/.968	Gwynn: - 21.06
11. Rice: - .5927	Waner - .974/.970	Waner: - 21.06
12. Flick: - .6185	Clemente - .973/.977	Musial: - 24.30
13. Youngs: - .646	Crawford - .972/.953	Ruth: - 24.30
14. Waner: - .6813	Jackson - .968/.977	Klein: - 30.78
15. Slaughter - .6821	Hooper - .967/.956	Flick: - 35.64
16. Guerrero: - .795	Ruth - .965/.963	Hooper: - 38.80
17. Keeler: -.800	Heilmann - .964/.962	Crawford: - 40.50
18. Thompson: - .854	Guerrero - .963/.981	Thompson: - 43.74
19. Robinson: - .9057	Klein - .963/.970	Slaughter: - .46.98
20. Jackson: - 1.021	Keeler - .960/.942	Rice: - 48.60
21. Heilmann: - 1.132	Youngs - .953/.962	Kelly: - 50.22
22. Crawford: - 1.23	Flick - .947/.949	Ott: - 51.84
23. Klein: - 1.24	Thompson - .934/.909	Keeler: - 56.70
24. Winfield: - 1.31	McCarthy - .897/.909	Youngs: - 61.56
25. McCarthy: - 1.74	Kelly - .820/.873	Heilmann: - 72.90

OBSERVATIONS AND COMMENTARY

Noticeable moves from JAWS to SAWS:

Aaron gets edged out by Musial for second place
Elmer Flick went from 15th to 7th
Sam Thompson went from 22st to 10th
King Kelly went from 23nd to 14th
Dave Winfield went from 13th to 24rd
Reggie Jackson went from 8th to 16th

60% of Babe Ruth's SAWS is 6.966 and eliminates all but four players. 60% of Musial's second highest score is 4.58 and only eliminates seven. Maybe the median of 5.04 (Tony Gwynn) should control.

1. <u>Babe Ruth – 1914-1935, WAR 1st, JAWS 1st</u>

   With Ruth in the room the only question in "who is in second place?" He is the only player to top 11 in SAWS and 11 in oWAR. Ted Williams comes in with a 10.10 in oWAR and he is the only other person with a double-digit score. And Ruth's 11 does not include his pitching WAR. The only offensive category listed above in which Ruth is not first is the SO/BB ratio. Remarkably he is third in dWAR so any stories about hiding him in right field because of his lousy fielding capabilities are bunk. Truly an "Immortal" but he came in second to Ty Cobb with a 95.1%.

2. <u>Stan Musial – 1939-1963, WAR 3rd, JAWS 3rd</u>

   Stan "the Man" edges Aaron out of second place because Hank hung on for two additional years as a DH. Stan is also second in oWAR by ½ of a game over Aaron. He is third in dWAR despite playing three positions (1B, LF, RF) not normally afforded much defensive respect. Musial is not without argument for being great. The biggest argument is where to slot him. Actually, he played more games at first base and left field but JAWS says his value is right field. So be it. He would have been second in left field and third at right field and ranks as the 13th greatest player under SAWS. Stan is second in six offensive first field comparison categories. He has a career slash line above .300/.400/.500, He is the only player with career rankings of 30 or greater in BA, OPB, SLG, OPS, OPS+, singles, doubles, triples, home runs, runs batted in, runs scored and total bases. And he missed one year to military duty. He had 28 league leaderships in the six main batting categories with three MVPs and 20 All-Star selections. Those league leaderships give him the ninth spot for dominance. And he only got 93.2% on his first ballot. Amazing.

3. <u>Hank Aaron – 1954-1976, WAR 2nd, JAWS 2nd</u>

   Most who hang on two years too long fall a lot farther than one slot. That is a testament to the superior play of Aaron. His oWAR is third and his dWAR is fourth so he was a complete player. Discussing his numbers or his credentials is really unnecessary. Excluding Barry Bonds, he is the leader in career home runs and runs batted in. He had seventeen league leaderships. He was one of only three right fielders who had a positive range factor above league. He had one MVP and 21 All-Star selections with his three Gold Gloves not to mention his 240 stolen bases. 3771 hits put him third all-time. Again, a disappointing 97.8% of the first ballot vote is all he received. I shudder to think that racism still played a role in 1981.

4. <u>Mel Ott – 1926-1947, WAR 4th, JAWS, 4th</u>

   Ott is another one of the few who break the .300/.400/.500 slash line, was the third player with 500+ homers and had 2876 hits. His oWAR is fourth and his dWAR is sixth so we are talking about another complete player. Offensively, his BA comes in at eighteenth, Otherwise, his two eighth place ranking in runs scored and SO/BB are the lowest he has. Although he was nine points above league fielding average he was 51 plays under the league range factor. He had fourteen league leaderships and eleven All-Star selections after they began in 1933. He was only third in thirteen MVP votes. I almost had to sit down when I saw that he was elected in his third ballot with a run-off vote of 87.2% in 1951.

5. Roberto Clemente – 1953-1972, WAR 6th, JAWS 6th

Clemente was known as a bad ball hitter and had a terrible SO/BB ratio which comes in 25th. But his low oWAR at 13th is a little unexpected especially with four league leaderships in BA. His comparative statistics validate the oWAR, though. He was eleventh in home runs, twelfth in SLG, sixteenth in runs created, seventeenth in OPS and OPS+, nineteenth in RBI, 22nd in runs scored and 23rd in OBP. His dWAR is first even though his fielding percentage was four points below league average. His throwing arm was legendary. He picked up twelve Gold Gloves after their inception in 1957. He had twelve All-Star selections and one MVP in twelve ballots. In two World Series he batted .362. He collected his 3000th hit and died tragically on an errand of mercy. He was elected immediately by special election and rightfully so.

6. Frank Robinson – 1956-1976, WAR 5th, JAWS 5th

Traded by Cincinnati at thirty years old as he was thought to be "over the hill," he went on to win his second MVP in another league. He also picked up a Triple Crown. At the fifth oWAR slot he is no stranger to upper level rankings in the comparisons. Rankings include third in home runs, fifth in OPS+, seventh in OPS, sixth in SLG, eighth in OBP, ninth in runs batted in, and thirteenth in runs scored. His dWAR at nineteen is not good but he is second in fielding percentage and ten points above league average. In any event his offense covers for it. He had 586 career home runs. He had thirteen league leaderships and thirteen All-Star selections. He was Rookie of the Year and eventually amassed 2943 hits with the help of 308 DH games. He won first ballot honors with 89.2%.

7. Elmer Flick – 1898-1910, WAR 18th, JAWS 15th

Here is a surprising name and a note that he only played thirteen seasons and 8.8992 effective seasons. That short career kept him eighteenth in WAR and fifteenth in JAWS, but SAWS compensates. A lot of knowledge about Flick can win a great number of bar room bets. He had the lowest BA for a batting championship in the AL at .308 until "Yaz" won his in 1968 with a .301. He was the oldest living inductee at 87. He wound out of baseball due to a stomach illness but lived to be 94. And the fact that Cleveland refused to trade him straight up for Ty Cobb is the trivia that got enough attention to get him enshrined in 1963 by the Veterans Committee. Prior to that he registered on one ballot in 1938 with .4% of the vote. He had four league leaderships in batting not counting two in stolen bases and three in triples. He was seventh in oWAR but his rankings do not support that. His OPS+ was sixth, OBP was ninth, BA was fourteenth, runs scored was fifteenth, OPS was eighteenth, as was SO/BB, SLG was nineteenth, runs batted in was twentieth, runs created was 21st, and home runs were 23rd. He was only twelfth in dWAR as his fielding percentage was two points below league average and his range factor was about 36 plays fewer than league average. He was sixth in OPS+ and ninth in OPB. I am in a quandary as to what to think but will give him his due in Cooperstown solely from his SAWS. His anecdotal life is fun to read about but irrelevant.

8. Harry Heilmann – 1914-1932, WAR, 11th, JAWS 9th

Offensively Heilmann comes in sixth in oWAR, That rank is understandable when you realize he was second in BA, fourth in OBP and RBI, fifth in OPS, sixth in runs created, seventh in OPS+ and eighth in in SLG. He was even thirteenth in home runs in a roomful of impressive sluggers. He breaks the career .300/.400/.500 slash line. Of his five league leaderships four were in BA and one was a .403. His dWAR was weak in 21st place with a last place standing in range factor. After thirteen ballots he found his way to 86.8% of the vote. I think the problem was he played in the American League at about the same time as The Babe. That was a big shadow.

9. Al Kaline – 1953-1974, WAR 7th, JAWS 7th

Kaline was not a superstar but he was one of the most consistent and complete players in the history of the game. Offensively his oWAR was only fourteenth and he had to scratch and claw his way to the median in the comparison categories. But he batted .297 with 399 home runs and 3007 hits although the last of those hits came the year he DHed for 147 games. His rankings are tenth in home runs, eleventh in SLG, twelfth in OPS, thirteenth in runs created, fifteenth in runs batted in, sixteenth in OBP and SO/BB and 20th in runs scored and batting average. His dWAR was second in the room with +6 percentage points on fielding and +24 plays on range factor. Ten Gold Gloves are understandable. He only had three league leaderships, but one was batting champion at the early age of twenty, still a record. He had fifteen All-Star appointments and came in second in one of his fourteen MVP ballots. He had a fantastic World Series in 1968 with a .371 BA, two homers and eight runs batted in. A first ballot winner with 88.3% of the vote. Agreed.

10. Sam Thompson – 1885-1906, WAR, 21st, JAWS 22nd

Thought by some to be the RBI champion with .9277 per game. However, if you use season adjustment to 162 nine-inning games Ruth comes in first with 158.57 versus 154.78 for Thompson. Thompson is not without credentials to discuss. Offensively he stays at tenth for oWAR, True to his era he was second in RBI and third in runs scored. He was fourth in runs created, sixth in BA, seventh in SO/BB, eighth in OPS+ and ninth in SLG and OPS. He had eight league leaderships and stole or advanced 232 bases. dWAR was not his shining light as he came in eighteenth with conflicting stats of 27 points above league in fielding and 44 fewer plays in range. Nary a vote until the 1974 Veterans Committee came along. This is a difficult one, but the numbers are there.

11. Paul Waner – 1926-1945, WAR 10th, JAWS 10th

The banners to wave for Waner are the 3152 hits and the .333 BA. Add a .404 OBP and he would be ushered into Cooperstown with 99% of the vote nowadays. Offensively and defensively he is a median Hall of Famer coming in eleventh in oWAR and fourteenth in dWAR. His offensive comparisons look better than eleventh place. He is second in SO/BB and fifth in BA and OBP. He is ninth in runs created and tenth in OPS and runs scored. He is fourteenth in OPS+ and fifteenth in SLG. His power stats of home runs come in eighteenth and runs batted in come in nineteenth. He collected one MVP in eight ballots and four All-Star selections after 1933. Three of his four league leaderships are batting average. He arrived on the seventh ballot with 83.3% of the vote. The hits, BA and OBP cannot be ignored and the seventh ballot is probably a little long to wait.

12. Sam Crawford – 1899-1917, WAR 8th, JAWS 11th

His nickname is more interesting than his statistics. "Yahoo Sam" comes in ninth in oWAR but his comparison rankings do not necessarily concur. I will not challenge the formulae for calculating oWAR in general, but something is amiss if traditional statistics and season adjustments differ from an oWAR calculation so much. Anyway, here they are. He is ninth is OPS+ and 14th in runs batted in. Then he is fifteenth in BA and SO/BB. He is eighteenth in SLG and nineteenth in home runs. Finally, we see 20th in OPS, 22nd in runs created and OPB, and 25th in runs scored. Forget his dWAR as it is 22nd in a room of 25. 309 triples is still the major league record but that record is peripheral at best. 367 stolen bases give slight improvement. With two HR league leaderships and three RBI league leaderships he had a little power for his era. A second in four MVP ballots does not ring my bell. He garnered all of 4.5% of the vote in seven BBWAA ballots and was then picked up by the Veterans Committee of 1957. Someone needs to explain this one to me.

13. Tony Gwynn – 1982-2001, WAR 12th, JAWS 12th

You must look completely past WAR, JAWS and SAWS to analyze Gwynn. Statistically, he is pure median, and the rankings confirm that. Take out his BA which was fourth and runs scored and runs batted in at 21st and the rest of his rankings range from tenth to sixteenth. But he was elected on his first ballot with 97.6%. He deserved it. His career BA was .338 and the best since Musial retired in 1963. That number ranks eighteenth in the history books. His only year with a BA under .300 was his rookie year. He has 3141 hits with only 15 DH games. He played for one team when he could have shopped around. He stole 319 bases. He was chosen for the All-Star team fifteen times. He won five Gold Gloves and seven Silver Sluggers. He was considered for twelve MVPs but only came in third once. Sometimes you cannot see the forest for the trees. This would have been one of those times if I wasn't careful.

14. King Kelly – 1878-1893, WAR 22nd, JAWS 23rd

King Kelly definitely had a high profile and could put on a show. He was a matinee idol and had a song to honor him. He was a swashbuckler to say the least. He was the image of baseball. Don't let the hype fool you though. He was more "show" than "go" when it comes to statistics. His oWAR was eighth but the comparison stats don't support it. He did score well in the runs scored category (second) but that was normal for his era and did have four league leaderships, two each in BA and OBP. Otherwise his OBP and runs created was 20th, his SLG and OPS was 21st. His OPS+ and RBI did come up to eleventh. His dWAR was also eighth but his fielding percentage was a whopping 53 percentage points below league average and his range factor was a negative 50.22 plays per season compared to league. The 1936 Veterans Committee showed him little support with a 19.2% vote, but the 1945 Old Timers Committee bought into his image. He was much more popular than great.

15. Vladimir Guerrero – 1996-2011, WAR 14th, JAWS 14th

Mostly a median player with power. His seasonal home runs are ranked fourth as is his SLG and his OPS. His season adjusted RBI count comes in seventh and his OPS+ comes in eighth but his oWAR overall comes in seventeenth. He was 23rd out of 25 in SO/BB because he swung at practically everything, but he did carry a BA of .318. He had no league leaderships in the six main batting categories. He collected one MVP in twelve votes and was chosen for nine All-Star squads. He ended with 2590 hits but used 508 DH games to get there. His fielding percentage was terrible at eighteen percentage points below league average. He rounded up 92.9% of the vote on the second ballot after 71.7% on the first ballot. I would not have come close to checking the box by his name, in either ballot. There was no *fame* or greatness.

16. Reggie Jackson – 1967-1987, WAR 9th, JAWS 8th

If there ever was a character with a high-profile image it was Reggie. But despite some unconvincing comparisons and rankings he earned his rewards. His oWAR comes in at sixteenth with fifth in season adjusted home runs being his best category. He stroked 563 in his career. BA was his worst area as he comes in last with a .262. He was twentieth in dWAR as his fielding percentage was nine points below league average. Hence the 630 games as DH. He holds the record for career strikeouts and came in next to last in seasonal strikeouts but only Reggie could make a strikeout exciting. He received fourteen All-Star appointments and one MVP out of thirteen considerations with two Silver Sluggers. He had ten league leaderships in the main batting categories. He even had a candy bar named after him. Now the good stuff. He played in five World Series, won four of them, was voted MVP in two of them, hit ten homers, three of them in one game and drove in 24 runs. Meet "Mr. October". He was a first ballot winner with 93.6%.

17. Enos Slaughter – 1938-1959, WAR 15th, JAWS 16th

His "Mad Dash" from first base to home plate in the 1946 World Series is still talked about as daring. His alleged intentional spiking of Jackie Robinson in 1947 is also still a topic of discussion or disdain. Enos did miss three prime years to military service and that did hurt his cumulative numbers, but he still got in nineteen seasons. He had moderate power but still ranks eighteenth in oWAR. His dWAR is only slightly better at fifteenth. Offensive rankings come in at tenth for runs batted in, thirteenth for OBP, fourteenth for home runs and runs created, sixteenth for OPS, seventeenth for SLG, eighteenth for runs scored, nineteenth for BA and 22nd for OPS+. Defensively he was two points above league fielding average but negative 42 compared to league range factor. He had one league leadership in RBI and only a second-place finish in eight MVP ballots. He did pull in ten All-Star appointments. In five World Series he batted .291. After fifteen BBWAA ballots he still fell short with 68.9% of the vote. The Veterans Committee of 1985 saw fit to enshrine him. Without the first two "events" he would be pretty much an unknown with good numbers. This is a close but no cigar situation.

18. Chuck Klein – 1928-1944, WAR 23rd, JAWS 21st

Klein came on like gangbusters early in his career winning four home run titles in his first six years. To top that off he won a Triple Crown in 1933. Of course, that was the apex of the "live ball" era and he did play in the Baker Bowl in Philadelphia which is slightly larger than a postage stamp. His power numbers lift him to twelfth in oWAR but almost all of his rankings are considerably higher than twelfth. In descending order, he was third in runs batted in and runs created, sixth in runs scored and seventh in home runs, eighth in OPS but thirteenth in OPS+ followed by fourteenth in OBP. His dWAR sinks to 23rd with seven points below league average in fielding and about 31 plays below league average in range factor. He only picked up one MVP, but two seconds in four looks, and two All-Star selections and he did have eleven league leaderships in the major batting categories – all by the age of 28. His votes on the thirteen writers' ballots lagged badly and topped at 27.9% but the 1980 Veterans Committee completed the process for him. Too much of a flash in the pan for me.

19. Ross Youngs – 1917-1926, WAR 24th, JAWS 24th

This man played ten seasons and was elected by the 1972 Veterans Committee after eighteen unsuccessful BBWAA ballots. He has no significant accomplishments to warrant a long discussion. His rankings are sixth in OBP and ninth in BA, thirteenth is SO/BB, fourteenth in runs scored and fifteenth in OPS. The rest of his rankings are between 18th and 22nd. His dWAR is thirteenth but his fielding percentage is nine points below league average and his range factor is 24th with 61.56 plays fewer than league average. I am not unsympathetic to his premature death at age 30 but this is uncalled for. Cronyism at its worst.

20. Willie Keeler – 1892-1910, WAR 16th, JAWS 17th

At 5'4" and a memorable mantra of "hit 'em where they ain't," he fulfills any requirement for being unique. He was first in SO/BB, third in BA, fourth in runs scored and eleventh in OBP but still found a lowly nineteenth spot for his oWAR thanks to a 20th in OPS+, a 22nd in OPS, a 23rd in SLG and a 24th in home runs and runs batted in. dWAR at seventeenth was not much better as his range factor compared to league was -57 but his fielding percentage was eighteen points higher than league average. 2932 hits from his .341 BA stands out. A .424 BA in 1897 does as well. But it is still a tight squeeze to put him in the Hall. I can live with a fifth ballot and 75.5%.

21. KiKi Cuyler – 1921-1938, WAR 20th, JAWS 20th

An unusual name and some slightly unusual rankings. His oWAR says 22nd but his individual comparisons beg to differ on occasion. His OPB and runs scored was seventh and his BA was tenth. His OPS and runs created came in at eleventh. His SLG was fourteenth and his home run rank was fifteenth, so he had a little power. His dWAR was much better at ninth and understandably so since he was eight points above league average in fielding and his range factor was sixth and only a -6. He had 328 stolen bases and led the league four times. He got to second place once in four MVP considerations. After twelve ballots with a top vote of 33.8% the 1968 Veterans Committee found him irresistible. I don't. He looks like a run of the mill "good" player.

22. Sam Rice – 1915-1934, WAR 19th, JAWS 18th

Rice is most frequently discussed in connection with a controversial catch in the 1925 World Series but just like Slaughter's "Mad Dash" it is not a true qualification for the Hall of Fame. He does rank eighth in BA and fourth in SO/BB ratio but otherwise you need to scroll down – way down – because he is 23rd overall in oWAR. Runs scored does figure in at twelfth but the rest range from 18th to 25th. He fared better at eleventh in dWAR but his range was 48.6 plays fewer per adjusted season than the league. He did steal 351 bases and led the league in SB once. He also led the league in caught stealing twice. He picked up one MVP in four ballots. It is difficult ignore a .322 BA and 2987 hits. After thirteen ballots ranging from .4% to 53% the 1963 Veterans Committee made it official. He has some good points in his favor, just not enough of them.

23. Harry Hooper – 1905-1925, WAR 17th, JAWS 19th

Offensive skills are close to nonexistent with Hooper. He checks in at 24th in BA, SLG, OPS and oWAR and that is the good news. He is last in runs created and RBI. On the flip side of the coin he was fifth in dWAR but only his fielding percentage agrees at nine points above league average. His range factor is -38. He came in 20th in one of two MVP votes. He did have 2466 hits and 375 stolen bases. In six ballots he scored all of 1.8% and the Veterans Committee of 1971 struck again. Absurd!

24. Dave Winfield – 1973-1995 excluding 1989, WAR 13th, JAWS 13th

Winfield should have never come back after leaving the game in 1988. He was in slightly over 700 games in his last six years and amassed 4.6 in WAR. So, his full record has him tumble from thirteenth in WAR and JAWS. His traditional or nonseason adjusted numbers do him no favors. He was 23rd in BA, last in OBP and nineteenth in OPS. He sank to 22nd in SO/BB. He scratched out all of one league leadership in RBI. He picked up twelve All-Star selections and seven Gold Gloves but, as mentioned much earlier, those can be partial popularity contests because he comes in 24th out of 25 in dWAR. He did, though, hit 465 homers and slap 3110 hits (thanks to a total of 419 games as DH and about 350 of them in his last five years) and writers tend to gush or drool over those statistics. And they did, rewarding him with a first ballot selection and 84.5%. I just cannot agree.

25. Tommy McCarthy – 1884-1896, WAR 25th, WAR 25th

Last and least, as he comes in dead last at 157th of all position players in WAR, JAWS, and SAWS successfully edging out Lloyd Waner is Tommy McCarthy. And he only played thirteen seasons and still could not advance under SAWS. His oWAR and dWAR are last place. All I can say about his statistics is that he had 469 stolen or advanced bases and led the league in that category one time. Stories abound about his inventiveness or advancement of play from the hit and run to sunglasses to fake bunts but those are credentials for pioneers not players. The Old Timers Committee of 1945 caused this one. Good grief!

STARTING PITCHERS

THE SEASONS

Actual	Effective
1. Nolan Ryan – 27	21.544
2. Steve Carlton – 24	20.8707
3. Phil Neikro – 24	21.616
4. Greg Maddux – 23	20.033
5. Don Sutton – 23	21.1293
6. Early Wynn – 23	18.256
7. Cy Young – 22	29.424
8. Randy Johnson – 22	16.5413
9. Bert Blyleven – 22	19.88
10. Gaylord Perry – 22	21.4
11. Tom Glavine – 22	17.6533
12. Red Ruffing – 22	17.3760
13. Herb Pennock – 22	14.2867
14. Walter Johnson – 21	23.6573
15. Warren Spahn – 21	20.184
16. Ted Lyons – 21	16.644
17. John Smoltz – 21	16.5551#
18. Eppa Rixey – 21	17.9787
19. Waite Hoyt – 21	15.0493
20. Pete Alexander – 20	20.76
21. Tom Seaver – 20	19.132
22. Red Faber – 20	16.3467
23. Ferguson Jenkins – 19	18.0027
24. Robin Roberts – 19	18.7547
25. Burleigh Grimes – 19	16.72
26. Jessie Haines – 19	12.8347
27. Pedro Martinez – 18	11.3093
28. Bob Feller – 18	15.308
29. Rube Marquard – 18	13.2267
30. Jack Morris – 18	15.2960
31. Lefty Grove – 17	15.7627
32. Bob Gibson – 17	15.5373
33. Christy Mathewson – 17	19.1547
34. Eddie Plank – 17	17.9827
35. Hal Newhouser – 17	11.9720
36. Jim Palmer – 17	15.7920
37. Jim Bunning – 17	15.0413

Actual	Effective
38. Dazzy Vance – 16	11.8667
39. Juan Marichal – 16	13.7987
40. Carl Hubbell – 16	14.3613
41. Whitey Ford – 16	12.6813
42. Chief Bender – 16	12.0680
43. Kid Nichols – 15	20.2680
44. Pud Galvin – 15	24.013
45. Catfish Hunter – 15	13.7973
46. Tim Keefe – 14	20.1987
47. Ed Walsh – 14	11.8573
48. Stan Coveleski – 14	12.3280
49. Don Drysdale – 14	13.728
50. Lefty Gomez – 14	9.9933
51. Mordecai Brown – 14	12.6893
52. Rube Waddell – 13	11.8444
53. Vic Willis – 13	15.984
54. Mickey Welch – 13	19.2080
55. Bob Lemon – 13	11.40
56. John Clarkson – 12	18.1453
57. Dizzy Dean – 12	7.8693
58. Sandy Koufax – 12	9.2973
59. Hoss Radbourn – 11	16.7373
60. Jack Chesbro – 11	11.5867
61. Amos Rusie – 10	15.1147
62. Joe McGinnity – 10	11.4427
63. Addie Joss – 9	9.308

Smoltz's effective seasons have been specifically calculated to reflect years as a starter and reliever.

THE RANKINGS

	SAWS	Pitching WAR	JAWS #
1.	Pedro Martinez – 7.622	Cy Young – 170	W Johnson – 127.4
2.	Lefty Grove – 7.137	W Johnson – 152.6	Cy Young – 123. 6
3.	Walter Johnson – 6.450	P Alexander – 117.3	K Nichols – 95.5
4.	Randy Johnson – 6.263	K Nichols – 116.6	P Alexander – 84.9
5.	Cy Young – 5.778	L Grove – 112.5	C Mathewson – 86.3
6.	Kid Nichols – 5.753	T Seaver – 106.3	L Grove – 85.8
7.	Sandy Koufax – 5.722	G Maddux – 104.9	T Seaver – 84.8
8.	Pete Alexander – 5.641	R Johnson – 103.6	G Maddux – 81.5
9.	Tom Seaver – 5.556	C Mathewson – 97.7	R Johnson – 81.3
10.	Dizzy Dean – 5.515	P Niekro – 97.3	J Clarkson – 79.5
11.	Ed Walsh – 5.381	B Blyleven – 96.6	T Keefe – 76.5
12.	Stan Coveleski – 5.297	G Perry – 93.4	W Spahn – 75.6
13.	Joe McGinnity – 5.287	W Spahn – 92.7	B Gibson – 75.4
14.	Dazzy Vance – 5.284	T Keefe – 88.8	P Niekro – 75.3
15.	Bob Gibson – 5.271	E Plank – 88.2	B Blyleven – 72.8
16.	Greg Maddux – 5.236	R Roberts – 88.1	S Carlton – 72.4
17.	Rube Waddell – 5.133	P Martinez – 86.2	G Perry – 71.5
18.	C. Mathewson – 5.101	J Clarkson – 85.8	H Radbourn – 71.3
19.	Hal Newhouser – 5.069	S Carlton – 88.4	E Plank – 71.2
20.	Addie Joss – 4.996	N Ryan – 84.1	P Martinez – 71.2
21.	Eddie Plank – 4.905	P Galvin – 83.3	R Roberts – 71.5
22.	Bert Blyleven – 4.859	F Jenkins – 82.4	F Jenkins – 67.9
23.	Carl Hubbell – 4.784	B Gibson – 81.9	P Galvin – 67.7
24.	John Clarkson – 4.729	T Glavine – 74.1	A Rusie – 67.6
25.	Warren Spahn – 4.593	H Radbourn – 73.1	E Walsh – 67.1
26.	Ferguson Jenkins – 4.577	C Hubbell – 68.7	N Ryan – 62.5
27.	Amos Rusie – 4.512	D Sutton – 68.6	T Glavine – 62.5
28.	Mordecai Brown – 4.507	R Faber – 68.5	M Welch – 58.6
29.	Phil Niekro – 4.501	A Rusie – 68.2	J Palmer – 58.3
30.	Juan Marichal – 4.486	J Palmer – 68.0	C Hubbell – 58.2
31.	Don Drysdale – 4.473	V Willis – 67.59	H Newhouser – 58.0
32.	Robin Roberts – 4.431	T Lyons – 67.58	B Feller – 57.9
33.	Tim Keefe – 4.396	J Smoltz – 66.5	J Marichal – 57.5
34.	Hoss Radbourn – 4.368	B Feller – 65.5	V Willis – 56.6
35.	Gaylord Perry – 4.365	S Coveleski – 65.3	T Lyons – 56.3
36.	Lefty Gomez – 4.313	E Walsh – 63.8	D Drysdale – 56.0

37. Jim Palmer – 4.306	M Welch – 63.6	S Coveleski – 55.1
38. Bob Feller – 4.279	D Vance – 62.7	J McGinnity – 55.0
39. Vic Willis – 4.229	J Marichal – 61.9	D Vance – 54.8
40. Whitey Ford – 4.227	D Drysdale – 61.4	R Ruffing – 54.5
41. Tom Glavine – 4.198	R Waddell – 60.8	J Bunning – 54.3
42. Red Faber – 4.190	H Newhouser – 60.7	R Waddell – 54.0
43. Ted Lyons – 4.062	J Bunning – 60.6	J Smoltz – 53.9
44. Steve Carlton – 4.044	J McGinnity – 60.5	R Faber – 52.9
45. Jim Bunning – 4.029	M Brown – 57.2	M Brown – 51.0
46. John Smoltz – 4.017	E Rixey – 56.8	D Sutton – 50.5
47. Nolan Ryan – 3.904	R Ruffing – 55.2	E Wynn – 49.8
48. Jack Chesbro – 3.616	W Ford – 53.6	S Koufax – 47.5
49. Chief Bender – 3.555	W Hoyt – 53.3	B Grimes – 46.9
50. Waite Hoyt – 3.542	S Koufax – 53.2	W Ford – 45.8
51. Pud Galvin – 3.469	E Wynn – 52	D Dean – 44.6
52. Bob Lemon – 3.316	B Grimes – 46.9	E Rixey – 44.5
53. Mickey Welch – 3.311	A Joss – 46.5	B Lemon – 43.5
54. Don Sutton – 3.247	J Morris – 44.0	W Hoyt – 43.1
55. Red Ruffing – 3.177	H Pennock – 43.9	A Joss – 41.5
56. Eppa Rixey – 3.159	D Dean – 43.4	J Chesbro – 41.3
57. Herb Pennock – 3.073	L Gomez – 43.1	C Bender – 40.9
58. Jack Morris – 2.877	C Bender – 42.4	H Pennock – 40.5
59. Early Wynn – 2.848	J Chesbro – 41.9	J Morris – 38.3
60. Burleigh Grimes – 2.805	B Lemon – 37.8	C Hunter – 38.1
61. Jesse Haines – 2.774	C Hunter – 36.6	L Gomez – 37.1
62. Catfish Hunter – 2.653	J Haines – 35.6	R Marquard – 30.9
63. Rube Marquard – 2.601	R Marquard – 34.4	J Haines – 27.2

The reader should specifically note that JAWS is calculated using WAR figures that include offensive and defensive WAR for a pitcher whereas SAWS is calculated using a 250-inning season and only pitching WAR. Figures will obviously differ, but many rankings of pitching WAR and JAWS still remain close.

TRADITIONAL STATISTICAL COMPARISONS

Wins	W/L %	Strikeouts
1. Cy Young – 511	W Ford - .690	N Ryan – 5714
2. Walter Johnson – 417	P Martinez - .687	R Johnson – 4875
3. Pete Alexander – 373	L Grove - .680	S Carlton – 4136

4. C Mathewson – 373	C Mathewson - .665	B Blyleven – 3701
5. Pud Galvin – 365	S Koufax - .655	T Seaver – 3640
6. Warren Spahn – 363	L Gomez - .649	D Sutton – 3574
7. Kid Nichols – 361	J Clarkson - .6482	G Perry – 3534
8. Greg Maddux – 355	M Brown - .6477	W Johnson – 3509
9. Tim Keefe – 342	R Johnson - .646	G Maddux – 3371
10. Steve Carlton – 329	D Dean - .644	P Niekro – 3342
11. John Clarkson – 328	P Alexander - .642	F Jenkins – 3192
12. Ed Plank – 326	Jim Palmer - .638	P Martinez – 3154
13. Nolan Ryan – 324	K Nichols - .6344	B Gibson – 3117
14. Don Sutton – 324	J McGinnity - .6340	J Smoltz – 3084
15. Phil Niekro – 318	J Marichal - .631	J Bunning – 2855
16. Gaylord Perry – 314	E Plank - .627	C Young – 2803
17. Tom Seaver – 311	C Bender - .625	T Glavine – 2607
18. Hoss Radbourn – 309	A Joss - .623	W Spahn – 2583
19. Mickey Welch – 307	C Hubbell - .622	B Feller – 2581
20. Tom Glavine – 305	B Feller - .621	T Keefe – 2564
21. Randy Johnson – 303	C Young - .6179	C Mathewson – 2597
22. Lefty Grove – 300	B Lemon - .6179	D Drysdale – 2486
23. Early Wynn – 300	H Radbourn - .614	J Morris – 2478
24. Bert Blyleven – 287	G Maddux - .610	S Koufax – 2396
25. Robin Roberts – 286	E Walsh - .607	R Roberts – 2357
26. Fergie Jenkins – 284	T Keefe - .6032	E Wynn – 2334
27. Red Ruffing – 273	T Seaver - .6027	R Waddell – 2316
28. Burleigh Grimes – 270	S Coveleski - .602	J Marichal – 2303
29. Jim Palmer – 268	T Glavine - .6004	L Grove – 2266
30. Bob Feller – 266	J Chesbro - .6000	E Plank – 2246
31. Eppa Rixey – 266	W Johnson - .599	J Palmer – 2212
32. Ted Lyons – 260	H Pennock - .598	P Alexander – 2198
33. Red Faber – 254	W Spahn - .597	D Vance – 2045
34. Jack Morris – 254	M Welch - .594	C Hunter – 2012
35. Carl Hubbell – 253	B Gibson - .591	R Ruffing – 1987
36. Bob Gibson – 251	A Rusie - .586	J Clarkson – 1978
37. Vic Willis – 249	D Vance - .585	W Ford – 1956
38. Amos Rusie – 246	H Newhouser - .580	A Rusie – 1950
39. Joe McGinnity – 246	J Smoltz - .579	K Nichols – 1881
40. Juan Marichal – 243	J Morris - .577	M Welch – 1850
41. Herb Pennock – 241	C Hunter - .5744	H Radbourn – 1830
42. Mordecai Brown – 239	R Waddell - .5744	P Galvin – 1807

43. Waite Hoyt – 237
44. Whitey Ford – 236
45. Jim Bunning – 224
46. Catfish Hunter – 224
47. Pedro Martinez – 219
48. Stan Coveleski – 215
49. John Smoltz – 213
50. Chief Bender – 212
51. Don Drysdale – 209
52. Jessie Haines – 209
53. Hal Newhouser – 207
54. Bob Lemon – 207
55. Rube Marquard – 201
56. Jack Chesbro – 198
57. Dazzy Vance – 197
58. Ed Walsh – 195
59. Rube Waddell – 193
60. Lefty Gomez – 189
61. Sandy Koufax – 165
62. Addie Joss – 160
63. Dizzy Dean – 150

S Carlton - .5742
J Haines - .571
W Hoyt - .566
B Grimes - .560
D Sutton - .559
D Drysdale - .5573
F Jenkins - .5569
E Wynn - .551
J Bunning - .549
V Willis - .5485
R Ruffing - .5482
R Faber - .544
G Perry - .542
P Galvin - .541
R Roberts - .539
P Niekro - .537
B Blyleven - .534
R Marquard - .532
T Lyons - .531
N Ryan - .526
E Rixey - .515

H Newhouser – 1796
E Walsh – 1736
C Bender – 1711
C Hubbell – 1677
V Willis – 1651
R Marquard – 1593
B Grimes – 1512
R Faber – 1471
L Gomez – 1468
M Brown – 1373
E Rixey – 1350
B Lemon – 1277
J Chesbro – 1265
H Pennock – 1227
W Hoyt – 1206
D Dean – 1163
T Lyons – 1073
J McGinnity – 1068
S Coveleski – 981
J Haines – 981
A Joss – 920

ERA

1. Ed Walsh – 1.82
2. Addie Joss – 1.89
3. Mordecai Brown – 2.06
4. Christy Mathewson – 2.13
5. Rube Waddell – 2.16
6. Walter Johnson – 2.17
7. Ed Plank – 2.35
8. Chief Bender – 2.46
9. Pete Alexander – 2.56
10. Cy Young – 2.63
11. Tim Keefe – 2.63
12. Vic Willis – 2.63
13. Joe McGinnity – 2.66
14. Hoss Radbourn – 2.68
15. Jack Chesbro – 2.68
16. Mickey Welch – 2.71

ERA+

P Martinez – 154
L Grove – 148
W Johnson – 147
E Walsh – 146
A Joss – 142
K Nichols – 140
M Brown – 139
C Young – 138
C Mathewson – 136
P Alexander – 135
R Johnson – 135
R Waddell – 135
J Clarkson – 133
W Ford – 133
G Maddux – 132
S Koufax – 131

WHIP

A Joss - .968
E Walsh – 1.0
P Martinez – 1.054
C Mathewson – 1.058
W Johnson – 1.061
M Brown – 1.066
J Marichal – 1.101
R Waddell – 1.102
S Koufax – 1.106
Chief Bender – 1.113
E Plank – 1.119
P Alexander – 1.121
T Seaver – 1.121
F Jenkins – 1.122
T Keefe – 1.123
C Young – 1.130

17. Whitey Ford – 2.75	D Dean – 131	C Hunter – 1.134
18. Sandy Koufax – 2.76	C Hubbell – 130	D Sutton – 1.142
19. John Clarkson – 2.81	H Newhouser – 130	G Maddux – 1.143
20. Pud Galvin – 2.85	A Rusie – 129	D Drysdale – 1.148
21. Tom Seaver – 2.86	T Seaver – 127	H Radbourn – 1.149
22. Jim Palmer – 2.86	B Gibson – 127	J Chesbro – 1.152
23. Juan Marichal – 2.89	S Coveleski – 127	C Hubbell – 1.166
24. Stan Coveleski – 2.89	Tim Keefe – 126	R Roberts – 1.17
25. Bob Gibson – 2.91	J Palmer – 125	R Johnson – 1.171
26. Pedro Martinez – 2.93	D Vance – 125	J Smoltz – 1.176
27. Don Drysdale – 2.95	J Smoltz – 125	J Bunning – 1.179
28. Kid Nichols – 2.96	L Gomez – 125	J Palmer – 1.18
29. Carl Hubbell – 2.98	J Marichal – 123	G Perry – 1.181
30. Dizzy Dean – 3.02	E Plank – 122	B Gibson – 1.188
31. Lefty Grove – 3.06	B Feller – 122	J McGinnity – 1.188
32. Hal Newhouser – 3.06	D Drysdale – 121	P Galvin – 1.191
33. Amos Rusie – 3.07	J McGinnity – 120	W Spahn – 1.195
34. Rube Marquard – 3.08	W Spahn – 119	B Blyleven – 1.198
35. Warren Spahn – 3.09	H Radbourn – 119	D Dean – 1.206
36. Gaylord Perry – 3.11	R Faber – 119	V Willis – 1.207
37. Red Faber – 3.15	B Lemon – 119	J Clarkson – 1.209
38. Eppa Rixey – 3.15	B Blyleven – 118	W Ford – 1.215
39. Greg Maddux – 3.16	T Glavine – 118	K Nichols – 1.224
40. Nolan Ryan – 3.19	V Willis – 118	M Welch – 1.226
41. Bob Lemon – 3.23	T Lyons – 118	D Vance – 1.23
42. Dazzy Vance – 3.24	G Perry – 117	R Marquard – 1.237
43. Bob Feller – 3.25	P Niekro – 115	S Carlton – 1.247
44. Don Sutton – 3.26	S Carlton – 115	N Ryan – 1.247
45. Catfish Hunter – 3.26	F Jenkins – 115	S Coveleski – 1.251
46. Jim Bunning – 3.27	J Bunning – 115	P Niekro – 1.268
47. Randy Johnson – 3.29	E Rixey – 115	E Rixey – 1.272
48. Bert Blyleven – 3.31	R Roberts – 113	L Grove – 1.278
49. Steve Carlton – 3.32	M Welch – 113	J Morris – 1.296
50. John Smoltz – 3.33	N Ryan – 112	R Faber – 1.302
51. Fergie Jenkins – 3.34	W Hoyt – 112	H Newhouser – 1.311
52. Lefty Gomez – 3.34	C Bender – 112	T Glavine – 1.314
53. Phil Niekro – 3.35	J Chesbro – 111	B Feller – 1.316
54. Robin Roberts – 3.41	R Ruffing – 109	E Wynn – 1.329
55. Burleigh Grimes – 3.53	J Haines – 109	B Lemon – 1.337

56. Tom Glavine – 3.54	D Sutton – 108	W Hoyt – 1.340
57. Early Wynn – 3.54	B Grimes – 108	R Ruffing – 1.341
58. Waite Hoyt – 3.59	P Galvin – 107	T Lyons – 1.348
59. Herb Pennock – 3.60	E Wynn – 107	H Pennock – 1.348
60. Jessie Haines – 3.64	H Pennock – 106	A Rusie – 1.349
61. Ted Lyons – 3.67	J Morris – 105	J Haines – 1.35
62. Red Ruffing – 3.80	C Hunter – 104	L Gomez – 1.352
63. Jack Morris – 3.90	R Marquard – 103	B Grimes – 1.365

SEASON ADJUSTED STATISTICAL COMPARISONS + TRADITIONAL SO/BB

	Wins/Season	SHO/Season	SO/Season	SO/BB
1.	McGinnity – 21.50	Joss – 4.83	RJohnson – 294.72	Martinez – 4.15
2.	Mathewson – 19.47	Walsh – 4.81	Martinez – 278.89	Maddux – 3.37
3.	Martinez – 19.36	WJohnson – 4.65	Ryan – 265.22	RJohnson – 3.26
4.	Dean – 19.06	Alexander – 4.34	Koufax – 257.71	Marichal – 3.25
5.	Grove – 19.03	Brown – 4.33	Gibson – 200.61	Jenkins – 3.20
6.	Gomez – 18.91	Koufax – 4.30	Carlton – 198.17	Smoltz – 3.05
7.	Brown – 18.83	Waddell – 4.22	Waddell – 195.54	Mathewson – 2.96
8.	Ford – 18.61	Mathewson – 4.12	Seaver – 190.26	Koufax – 2.93
9.	Radbourn – 18.46	Plank – 3.84	Bunning – 189.81	Drysdale – 2.91
10.	RJohnson – 18.32	Marichal – 3.77	Smoltz – 186.29	Waddell – 2.88
11.	Lemon – 18.16	Gibson – 3.60	Blyleven – 186.17	Bunning – 2.85
12.	Plank – 18.13	Drysdale – 3.57	Drysdale – 181.09	Walsh – 2.81
13.	Clarkson – 18.08	Ford – 3.55	Jenkins – 177.31	Blyleven – 2.80
14.	Spahn – 17.98	Palmer – 3.36	Vance – 172.33	Sutton – 2.66
15.	Alexamder – 17.97	Bender – 3.31	Sutton – 169.15	Seaver – 2.62
16.	Nichols – 17.81	Dean – 3.30	Feller – 168.60	Roberts – 2.61
17.	Koufax – 17.75	Seaver – 3.19	Maddux – 168.27	WJohnson – 2.574
18.	Maddux – 17.72	Willis – 3.13	Marichal – 166.90	Dean – 2.567
19.	WJohnson – 17.63	Spahn – 3.12	Perry – 165.14	Perry – 2.56
20.	Hubbell – 17.62	Coveleski – 3.08	Morris – 162.00	Joss – 2.53
21.	Marichal – 17.61	Hunter – 3.04	Niekro – 154.61	Vance – 2.434
22.	Bender – 17.57	Chesbro – 3.02	Ford – 154.24	Galvin – 2.426
23.	Coveleski – 17.44	Blyleven – 3.02	Newhouser – 150.02	Bender – 2.40
24.	Feller – 17.38	Feller – 2.87	WJohnson – 148.33	Gibson – 2.33
25.	Young – 17.37	Ryan – 2.83	Dean – 147.79	Hubbell – 2.313
26.	Newhouser – 17.29	Gomez – 2.801	Glavine – 147.68	Alexander – 2.311

27. Glavine – 17.28	McGinnity – 2.796	Gomez – 146.90	Young – 2.30
28. Joss – 17.19	Newhouser – 2.76	Walsh – 146.41	Carlton – 2.26
29. Chesbro – 17.09	Sutton – 2.74	Hunter – 145.83	Hunter – 2.21
30. Palmer – 16.97	Jenkins – 2.721	Grove – 143.75	Plank – 2.10
31. Keefe – 16.93	Lemon – 2.719	Bender – 141.78	Radbourn – 2.09
32. Pennock – 16.86	Wynn – 2.68	Palmer – 140.07	Keefe – 2.08
33. Smoltz – 16.70	Bunning – 2.66	Mathewson – 130.88	Ryan – 2.044
34. Morris – 16.61	Carlton – 2.64	Rusie – 129.01	Brown – 2.043
35. Vance – 16.60	Ruffing – 2.59	Spahn – 127.97	Grove – 1.91
36. Walsh – 16.45	Young – 2.58	Wynn – 127.85	Marquard – 1.86
37. Wynn – 16.43	Hubbell – 2.51	Keefe – 126.94	Niekro – 1.85
38. Haines – 16.36	Perry – 2.48	Roberts – 125.68	Chesbro – 1.83
39. Waddell – 16.29	Pennock – 2.45	Plank – 124.90	Spahn – 1.8013
40. Rusie – 16.28	Vance – 2.44	Marquard – 120.44	Ford – 1.8011
41. Seaver – 16.26	Roberts – 2.40	Hubbell – 116.77	Morris – 1.78
42. Hunter – 16.24	Galvin – 2.37	Ruffing – 114.35	Glavine – 1.74
43. Gibson – 16.154	Nichols – 2.37	Lemon – 112.02	Palmer – 1.69
44. Grimes – 16.148	Marquard – 2.27	Radbourn – 109.34	Clarkson – 1.66
45. Welch – 15.98	RJohnson – 2.24	Chesbro – 109.18	Nichols – 1.48
46. Jenkins – 15.78	Grove – 2.22	Brown – 108.36	Feller – 1.46
47. Carlton – 15.76	Welch – 2.13	Alexander – 105.88	Newhouser – 1.44
48. Hoyt – 15.75	Grimes – 2.093	Willis – 103.29	Welch – 1.43
49. Ruffing – 15.71	Radbourn – 2.091	Clarkson – 103.01	Willis – 1.36
50. Lyons – 15.62	Niekro – 2.08	Joss – 99.84	Gomez – 1.341
51. Willis – 15.58	Rixey – 2.06	Welch – 96.31	Pennock – 1.339
52. Faber – 15.54	Clarkson – 2.04	Young – 95.26	McGinnity – 1.32
53. Sutton – 15.33	Rusie – 1.98	McGinnity – 93.33	Wynn – 1.31
54. Roberts – 15.25	Keefe – 1.93	Nichols – 92.81	Ruffing – 1.29
55. Drysdale – 15.22	Morris – 1.83	Grimes – 90.43	Rixey – 1.25
56. Galvin – 15.200	Haines – 1.79	Faber – 89.99	Coveleski – 1.22
57. Marquard – 15.196	Faber – 1.77	Pennock – 85.88	Faber – 1.21
58. Ryan – 15.04	Maddux – 1.75	Hoyt – 80.14	Hoyt – 1.20
59. Bunning – 14.89	Hoyt – 1.73	Coveleski – 79.58	Grimes – 1.17
60. Rixey – 14.80	Lyons – 1.62	Haines – 76.43	Rusie – 1.14
61. Niekro – 14.71	Martinez – 1.50	Galvin – 75.25	Haines – 1.13
62. Perry – 14.67	Glavine -1.42	Rixey – 75.09	Lemon – 1.02
63. Blyleven – 14.44	Smoltz – 1.25	Lyons – 64.47	Lyons - .96

OBSERVATIONS AND COMMENTARY

Noticeable moves from JAWS to SAWS:

Pedro Martinez goes from 20th to 1st

Sandy Koufax goes from 48th to 7th

Dizzy Dean goes from 51st to 10th

Stan Coveleski goes from 37th to 12th

J. McGinnity goes from 48th to 13th

Dazzy Vance goes from 39th to 14th

Rube Waddell goes from 42nd to 17th

Addie Joss goes from 55th to 20th

Mord. Brown goes from 45th to 25th

Lefty Gomez goes from 61st to 36th

Greg Maddux goes from 8th to 16th

Christy Mathewson goes from 5th to 18th

Warren Spahn goes from 12th to 25th

Phil Niekro goes from 14th to 29th

Tim Keefe goes from 11th to 33rd

Hoss Radbourn goes from 18th to 34th

Gaylord Perry goes from 17th to 35th

Tom Glavine goes from 27th to 41st

Steve Carlton goes from 16th to 44th

Nolan Ryan goes from 26th to 47th

The 60% SAWS cutoff is 4.573. The median is Robin Roberts at 4.431

1. <u>Pedro Martinez – 1992-2009, WAR 17th, JAWS 20th</u>

   Many may be uncomfortable with Martinez leaping to first place above traditional names. Some will point to how SAWS benefits shorter careers and Martinez did play eighteen seasons but only 13.3 effective seasons. It does benefit shorter careers but only if the quality is there. And Martinez has the quality. He is first in ERA+ and SO/BB ratio. He is second in won-loss percentage and second in season adjusted strikeouts. He is third in WHIP and season adjusted wins. He had nine league leaderships in ERA, wins and strikeouts, the three prongs of the Triple Crown. That makes him tenth in what I call the dominance factor for pitchers. (See Additional Pitcher Comparisons at the end of Position Player Consolidations). He won three Cy Young Awards and was second in another vote. He was chosen for eight All-Star Games. He was elected on the first ballot with 91.1%. A no-brainer.

2. Lefty Grove – 1925-1941, WAR 5th, JAWS 6th

Yet another pitcher outperforming Walter Johnson and Cy Young. His won-loss percentage ranks third. His ERA+ ranks second. His season adjusted wins ranks fifth. He is only 30th in strikeouts but he led the league seven times. He is 35th in SO/BB but he led the league eight times. He is 48th in WHIP but he led the league five times. He had twenty league leaderships in the Triple Crown categories and two Triple Crowns. Those twenty league leaderships make him the second most dominant pitcher in the history of the game. He won one MVP from eight votes and was elected to six of the first seven All-Star games. Astoundingly he was not elected until his fifth ballot with only 76.4%. SAWS, JAWS and WAR shows you how writers can get it all wrong.

3. Walter Johnson – 1909-1927, WAR 2nd, JAWS 1st

He is the pitcher most would say is number one in the history of the game and by JAWS he is. He is second in wins with 417 even while playing for a second division team most of his career. He is nineteenth in season adjusted wins. His ERA+ comes in fourth and his ERA comes in at sixth. He is fifth in WHIP, but he led the league six times. He is first in shutouts but third in season adjusted shutouts. He is eighth in strikeouts but 24th in season adjusted strikeouts. He is seventeenth in strikeouts to base on balls ratio. He had 23 league leaderships in ERA, strikeouts and wins but came in fourth in season adjusted league leaderships showing dominance. He won two MVPs and threw one no-hitter. He won three Triple Crowns. Yes, he was "Immortal" with 83.6% of the vote.

4. Randy Johnson – 1988-2009, WAR 8th, JAWS 9th

He is first in season adjusted strikeouts, second in career strikeouts and third in SO/BB. He is ninth in won-loss percentage, tenth in adjusted wins per season and eleventh in ERA+. He had fourteen league leaderships in the Triple Crown categories and that gives him sixth position in dominance. He does falter in WHIP where he comes in 25th but he did lead the league three times. He has one no-hitter, one perfect game and one Triple Crown. He won five Cy Young Awards and received ten appointments to the All-Star teams. He was sixth once in nine MVP votes. He was 3-0 in the 2001 World Series and named Series MVP. He finished with 303 wins in 21st place all-time. He was a first ballot winner with 97.3% of the vote.

5. Cy Young – 1890-1911, WAR 1st, JAWS 2nd

Many would choose Young as the greatest as he had the most wins and the highest WAR. But under SAWS he falls quite a bit and fifth place could actually be called a third tier of greatness since the first two had 7+ wins and the second two had 6+ wins and Young only has 5.7. He was eighth in ERA+ and only had nine league leaderships.

He was fifteenth in WHIP, but he led the league seven times. He was 21st in won-loss percentage. Despite his 511 wins he was 25th in season adjusted wins. He was 27th in SO/BB but he led the league eleven times due to leading the league fourteen times in walks. For an old timer when shutouts ruled he was only 36th in shutouts per season. He was 52nd in strikeouts per season. Longevity makes him the career leader in eight categories. He was elected in 1937 with 76.1%.

6. Kid Nichols – 1890-1906, WAR 4th, JAWS 3rd

The biggest and most reported story about Kid Nichols is that Ty Cobb gave him a great plug as a pitcher. Otherwise, Nichols may never have been elected or at least would have been elected far later. The 1936 Veterans Committee and the BBWAA gave him from .5% to 3.8% before the Old Timers Committee of 1949 picked up on him. He did seem to be very unassuming and lost in the shuffle with Johnson, Mathewson and Young. I never figured out how Cobb knew much about his actual pitching except for statistics since Nichols finished his career in the National League in 1906 pitching all of four games and Cobb started his career in the American League in 1905. Anyway, Nichols has some redeeming qualifications. He was seventh with 361 wins and won 30 games seven times. He led the league three times in wins but never in ERA or strikeouts and is only one of eight pitchers in the Hall to never win two prongs of the Triple Crown. He was thirteenth in won-loss percentage. He was sixth in ERA+. He was 39th in WHIP but led the league three times and 39th in career strikeouts but 54th in season adjusted strikeouts. He was 45th in SO/BB ratio. I am not impressed.

7. Sandy Koufax – 1955-1966, WAR 50th, JAWS 48th

Argued by many as the greatest pitcher ever to have graced the major leagues so a ranking system that puts him 50th or 48th out of 63 needs some adjustment. He had twelve league leaderships in the Triple Crown categories and comes in first for season adjusted league leaderships and dominance. He came in fourth in won-loss percentage. He may have come in 24th in career strikeouts but he comes in fourth in season adjusted strikeouts, one of only four to register more than 250 per adjusted season. He was sixth in season adjusted shutouts and the first pitcher to notch four or more since Walter Johnson retired. He was eighth in SO/BB ratio and led the league three times. He was ninth in WHIP and led the league four times and only eleven other Hall of Fame pitchers have led four or more times. He was sixteenth in ERA+ and seventeenth in season adjusted wins. He won three Major League Cy Young Awards and won a concurrent MVP with two second places. He threw three no-hitters and one perfect game. In World Series play of 57 innings he has 61 strikeouts, a WHIP of .825 and an ERA of .91 in addition to being named MVP twice. Elected on the first ballot with only 86.9% of the vote can only indicate how a short career hurts.

8. Grover Cleveland "Pete" Alexander – 1911-1930, WAR 3rd, JAWS 4th

He is third in wins but only fifteenth in season adjusted wins. He may be 32nd in career strikeouts and 47th in season adjusted strikeouts but he led the league six times. He was tenth in ERA+ and eleventh in won-loss percentage. He was twelfth in WHIP but led the league four times. He was fourth in season adjusted shutouts and led the league seven times. He was 26th in SO/BB ratio but led the league three times. He was seventh overall in season adjusted league leaderships of the three main categories for the Triple Crown and should be considered very dominant. Speaking of Triple Crowns, he won it in three consecutive years. He only came in third in six MVP ballots. He was a third ballot choice with 80.9%.

9. Tom Seaver – 1967-1986, WAR 6th, JAWS 7th

He won 311 games but only garnered 41st in adjusted season wins. He was 27th in won-loss percentage and 21st in ERA+. He is fifteenth in SO/BB ratio but led the league three times. He was seventeenth in season adjusted shutouts and led the league twice. He was thirteenth in WHIP and led the league three times. He dominance rank was sixteenth from eleven season adjusted Triple Crown league leaderships. He was eighth in season adjusted strikeouts and fifth in total strikeouts. He did lead the league five times in the strikeout category. Awards were plentiful as he started with Rookie of the Year and progressed to twelve All-Star appointments and then to three Cy Young Awards with two seconds and ten MVP considerations. To put it bluntly, he was terrific. 98.8% on the first ballot held the honors until Griffey.

10. Dizzy Dean – 1930-1941,1947, WAR 56th, JAWS 51st

If votes for the Hall of Fame were based solely on image, Dean would have received 100%. He was dead last in wins with 150 but he was fourth in season adjusted wins ahead of every pitcher above him in SAWS but Martinez. And he only trailed Pedro by .3 games per adjusted season. He was tenth in won-loss percentage. Sliding down the slope he stops at sixteenth for season adjusted shutouts while leading the league in shutouts twice. A slight slip leaves his ERA+ at seventeenth. He was 25th in season adjusted strikeouts but led the league in that category four times. He took a plunge to 35th in WHIP. He corralled one MVP and two second place votes with his four All-Star selections, one of which turned out to be a disaster. The BBWAA did not think much of him as it took eleven ballots before he climbed to 79.2%. But they did not have WAR or JAWS, or more importantly SAWS.

11. Ed Walsh – 1904-1917, WAR 36th, JAWS 25th

A fourteen-season career was adjusted to 11.8573 seasons but contained some impressive numbers. Enough to elevate him quite a bit in rank. He starts off slowly but picks up some steam. He was 58th in wins but climbed to 36th in season adjusted wins. His 44th in strikeouts became 28th in season adjusted strikeouts. His won-loss percentage stays at 25th. He was twelfth in SO/BB ratio. He was first in ERA with 1.82 and fourth in ERA+. He was second in WHIP. He was second in season adjusted shutouts and led the league in shutouts three times. He threw one no-hitter and he placed second in MVP votes two times. It took the 1946 Old Timers Committee to help him along after eight ballots with a top of 56.9%. This may be one of the better moves of the 1946 Committee.

12. Stan Coveleski – 1912-1928. WAR 35th, JAWS 37th

Seventeen actual years and fourteen actual seasons resulted in only 12.328 effective seasons which allows SAWS to shine more light on him. Too much, in my opinion. He was 48th in wins and 23rd in season adjusted wins. He was 28th in won-loss percentage and 23rd in ERA+. He did scale to twentieth in season adjusted shutouts. Now for the bad stuff. He sank to 45th in WHIP. He floundered at 60th in strikeouts and 59th in season adjusted strikeouts. Following in those cricles he was 56th in SO/BB ratio. Don't blame SAWS. Better yet ask how he accumulated 65.3 WAR in such a short time. After five writers' ballots with a maximum of 12.8% of the vote the 1969 Veterans Committee threw him a lifeline. Something is amiss here.

13. Joe McGinnity – 1899-1908, WAR 44th, JAWS 48th

Nicknamed the "Iron Man" because of a family business but it suits him just fine on the field as ten years is a very short period of time to do what he did and that is what explains his almost meteoric rise. He led the league six times in appearances and four times in innings pitched and twice in batters faced. But those aren't the numbers that should get you dubbed as famous. He did have six wins in the Triple Crown categories, all in wins, but no Triple Crown. That sure doesn't justify moving from 44th in WAR and 38th in JAWS to his current view from above. He was 39th in wins but a remarkable first in season adjusted wins and he is the only pitcher in the history of the game to log more than twenty. He was fourteenth in won-loss percentage. It doesn't get any better. He was 27th in season adjusted shutouts and 31st in WHIP. He was thirteenth in ERA but that had serious adjustment to the park and league which left him 33rd in ERA+. He came in 52nd in SO/BB ratio, 53rd in season adjusted strikeouts and 60th in strikeouts. After seven ballots wrapping up all of 26.2% of the vote the 1946 Old Timers Committee committed this sin.

14. Dazzy Vance – 1915, 1918, 1922-1935, WAR 38th, JAWS 39th

From way down the line comes Vance. He had twelve league leaderships in strikeouts, ERA and wins which with his 11.8667 effective seasons pole vaults him to third in season adjusted league leaderships which renders him dominant. The rest is a mixed bag. He was fourteenth in season adjusted strikeouts and 21st in his strikeout to base on ball ratio so he bedazzled a few with his fastball. He was 26th in ERA+ and 41st in WHIP but led the league in WHIP three times. He was below median in won-loss percentage at 37th. We find him even further down at 57th in wins. But he crawled up to 35th in season adjusted wins. He picked up one MVP in three ballots. Ballots were practically his middle name with seventeen of them while his vote count climbed from .4% to 81.7%. I do not understand this one at all.

15. Bob Gibson – 1959-1975, WAR 23rd, JAWS 13th

He is 36th in wins, 35th in won-loss percentage, and drops to 43rd in season adjusted wins. He only improves slightly to 30th in WHIP, 24th in SO/BB and 22nd in ERA+. A few more rungs up the ladder and we find him at eleventh in season adjusted shutouts which is high for any pitcher not close to the nineteenth century. He has two Cy Youngs and one MVP in 1968 when he threw thirteen shutouts, tied for third all-time, and posted a 1.12 ERA which is fourth all-time. He was selected to eight All-Star squads. Nine Gold Gloves and 24 home runs with the bat show he could field and hit. But it is his World Series play that is still talked about. Nine starts, eight complete games, seven wins with 92 strikeouts in 81 innings, seventeen of them in one game and 35 in one Series with two Series MVPs. The single game and single Series numbers are still records. First ballot selection with 84%. Way too low in my opinion.

16. Greg Maddux – 1986-2008, WAR 7th, JAWS 8th

Maddux falls to this position because he hung on just a little too long. He is eighth in career wins, 18th in season adjusted wins and 24th in won-loss percentage. He is ninth in career strikeouts and seventeenth in season adjusted strikeouts but second in SO/BB ratio primarily because he led the league in fewest walks nine times. It is interesting to note that Maddux had about twenty more season adjusted strikeouts than Walter Johnson. His ERA is 39th but he led the league four times. His ERA+ is fifteenth. His WHIP is nineteenth, but he also led the league four times there as well. He picked up four Cy Young Awards and came in second once and third twice. He received eight All-Star appointments and was considered for MVP six times. Most notably he collected eighteen Gold Gloves. His post season performance was lackluster but that doesn't count in calculations. First ballot selection with 97.2%.

17. Rube Waddell – 1897, 1899-1910, WAR 41st, JAWS 42nd

Another short career but one full of credentials for the Hall of Fame. Obviously, his number of wins comes in with a poor rank of 59th but so does his season adjusted wins at 39th and his won-loss percentage at 42nd. He is 28th in strikeouts but his season adjusted strikeouts rank seventh and he is the highest-ranking pitcher from the turn of the twentieth century. He did lead the league in strikeouts six times. His SO/BB ratio is tenth. His ERA+ is twelfth while his WHIP is eighth. He was also a shutout pitcher as he ranked seventh in season adjusted shutouts. He led the league nine times in Triple Crown categories and placed ninth in dominance while winning one Triple Crown. Eight rejections by the writers was remedied by the 1946 Old Timers Committee which was one of their few good choices.

18. Christy Mathewson – 1900-1916, WAR 9th, JAWS 5th

One can easily argue that SAWS has it all wrong with Mathewson at this slot since he was the first pitcher, an "Immortal," to be elected and with a 90.7% vote. But his full record includes 1914-1916 when his health obviously hurt his score. Without those three years he would have probably been ranked about eleventh. He was great. Tied for third in career wins and second in season adjusted wins with fourth place for won-loss percentage is a pretty good start for fame. He was 21st in strikeouts but he led the league five times. He was 33rd in season adjusted strikeouts but a strong seventh in SO/BB ratio as he led the league nine times in that category. Continuing with the kudos he is fourth in WHIP with five league leaderships, ninth in ERA+ with six leaderships and eighth in season adjusted shutouts. He collected two Triple Crowns and threw two no hitters. He was twelfth in dominance ranking. Easy choice.

19. Hal Newhouser – 1939-1955, WAR 42nd, JAWS 31st

His seventeen seasons only yielded 11.972 effective seasons and moves him up considerably from WAR and JAWS. An eleven rank move with JAWS tells me he had some strong years to be averaged in. His comparative statistics and rankings are somewhat "good news – bad news." He is 53rd in wins but 26th in season adjusted wins. His won-loss percentage is 38th. His strikeouts rank 43rd but move up to 23rd with season adjustment. His SO/BB stays at 47th. He is nineteenth in ERA+ but 51st in WHIP. He is 28th in season adjusted shutouts. He came in fourteenth in dominance and won one Triple Crown while picking up two MVPs. He landed six All-Star games. After fourteen BBWAA votes reaching 42% the 1992 Veterans Committee liked him. I can see it.

20. Addie Joss – 1902-1910, WAR 53rd, JAWS 55th

Due to his premature death the ten-year requirement was obviously waived since Joss only pitched nine years. His won-loss percentage was eighteenth and his season adjusted wins comes in 28th. His strikcouts are weak at 63rd but he rises slightly to 50th with season adjustment. He is stronger in SO/BB with a 20th ranking. His strengths are many. He was first in WHIP and season adjusted shutouts. He was second in ERA and fifth in ERA+. He threw one no-hitter and one perfect game. After seven ballots with a maximum of 14.2% the 1978 Veterans Committee did the right thing. Coming from so far down in WAR and JAWS seems appropriate to me to accent quality.

21. Eddie Plank – 1901-1917, WAR 15th, JAWS 19th

There is so little to talk about with Plank. He was consistent as he was twelfth in wins, twelfth in season adjusted wins, eleventh in WHIP, ninth in season adjusted shutouts and tenth in won-loss percentage. He was seventh in ERA but 30th in ERA+. Strikeouts were not his forte as he was 30th in career strikeouts, 39th in season adjusted strikeouts and 30th in SO/BB. He had no league leaderships in wins, ERA or strikeouts. He and Mickey Welch, Chief Bender, Herb Pennock and Jesse Haines carry that distinction. In four World Series he went 2-5. Six writers' ballots gave him 26% but the 1946 Old Timers Committee seemed to like him. They must have been impressed with his 326 wins or felt sorry for him being so overshadowed by Johnson, Young and Mathewson. I am very unsure about this player despite his rankings.

22. Bert Blyleven – 1970-1990, 1992, WAR 11th, JAWS 15th

WAR has him as the eleventh greatest pitcher which I cannot fathom. Even his JAWS rating at fifteenth is highly questionable for me. SAWS at 22nd is still a puzzle. Blyleven pitched for a long, long time and accumulated a lot of numbers. Some of them are even good, but most aren't. Fourth in strikeouts, eleventh in season adjusted strikeouts and thirteenth in SO/BB ratio are the good ones. He threw one no-hitter. That is it. He is 24th in wins but dead last in season adjusted wins and 59th out of 63 in won-loss percentage. He came in dead last in winning only 41.9% of his starts. He is 48th in ERA and 38th in ERA+ while slotting in at 34th in WHIP. He was given four looks for a Cy Young award and came in third twice. He was chosen for the All-Star game twice and lodged a thirteenth place in two MVP votes. He led the league in losses one year. It took him fourteen ballots to climb from a low of 14.1% to 79.7%. No check by his name from me.

23. Carl Hubbell – 1928-1943, WAR 26th, JAWS 30th

Known for a screwball and a debatable consecutive win streak. He had seven league leaderships in ERA, wins and strikeouts but fell just short of the upper echelons of dominance. He threw one no-hitter and won a Triple Crown. He also had two MVPs out of six looks and found the All-Star roster nine times after 1933. Some numerical reality is that he is 35th in wins, twentieth in season adjusted wins and 19th in won-loss percentage. He is 29th in ERA and eighteenth in ERA+ while falling in at 23rd in WHIP but he had six league leaderships in WHIP. His strikeout numbers are not as impressive as he is 46th in career strikeouts, 41st in season adjusted strikeouts and 25th in SO/BB ratio. It only took him four BBWAA ballots to go from 9.7% to 87%. I would vote for him, but I will never understand the vote climbing that way.

24. John Clarkson – 1882, 1884-1893, WAR 18th, JAWS 10th

Now the discussion really gets tough. Pitching in his era is so different than it is now, or for that matter, was twenty years after he retired. He had some impressive numbers though. He was eleventh in wins, thirteenth in season adjusted wins and seventh in won-loss percentage. He is nineteenth in ERA and thirteenth in ERA+ and 37th in WHIP. Strikeout numbers are below median. He was 36th in strikeouts, 49th in season adjusted strikeouts and 44th in SO/BB. He had seven league leaderships, but just like Hubbell, falls short of dominance. He tossed one no-hitter and snared one Triple Crown. The 1936 Veterans Committee gave him a thumbs-down with 6.4% of the vote. It wasn't until 1963 that the Veterans Committee revisited his name and elected him. Knowing what I know now I would vote for him.

25. Warren Spahn – 1942, 1946-1965, WAR 13th, JAWS 12th

Spahn takes a fall in WAR and JAWS primarily due to the fact that he was never a superstar pitcher when it came to WAR. He was consistently very good for a long, long time. He is the winningest lefthander in the history of the game and ranks sixth. He is also fourteenth in season adjusted wins but only 33rd in won-loss percentage. He was eighteenth in career strikeouts but only 35th in season adjusted strikeouts and only 39th in SO/BB ratio. He is definitely median in ERA, ERA+ and WHIP with ranks of 35th, 34th and 33rd, respectively. He was, though, nineteenth in season adjusted shutouts which is good for someone pitching into the 1960s. He led the league fifteen times in ERA, wins and strikeouts and comes in eleventh in dominance. He was amazingly durable as he started 32-41 games for eighteen consecutive years. He picked up one Cy Young award and came in second three times and third once. He joined the All-Star roster fourteen times and was considered in fifteen MVP votes. All this and he missed over three seasons to military duty in WWII. Ignoring a single vote in 1958 he was elected in his first ballot with 83.2%. A clear Hall of Famer.

26. Fergie Jenkins – 1965-1983, WAR 22nd, JAWS, 22nd

He is another "good news-bad news" pitcher. He is fifth in SO/BB ratio, eleventh in strikeouts, thirteenth in season adjusted strikeouts, and seventeenth in WHIP. Then he ranks 26th in wins, 30th in season adjusted shutouts, 45th in ERA+, 46th in season adjusted wins, 49th in won-loss percentage, and 51st in ERA. He had one Cy Young award out of six votes but came in second twice. He only saw six MVP ballots with his name on them and only joined three All-Star teams. He gave up 484 home runs in his career which is third all-time. He slipped in on his third ballot with 75.4%. I cannot agree despite his 284 wins.

27. Amos Rusie – 1889-1901, WAR 29th, JAWS 24th

The "Hoosier Thunderbolt" slipped in his tenth year by returning to the majors to pitch in three games in 1901. In his first six years with the New York Giants he led the league in strikeouts five times and walks five times and wild pitches once. He was not a good control pitcher. He led the league once in wild pitches. I can only imagine the fear that put into batters with his nickname coming from his fastball. His traditional statistics as well as his season adjusted statistics are not that good and many are below median. He is 38th in wins, 36th in won-loss percentage, 38th in strikeouts, 60th in SO/BB ratio, 33rd in ERA but 20th in ERA+, and 51st in WHIP. He is 40th in season adjusted wins, 53rd in season adjusted shutouts, and 34th in season adjusted strikeouts. He is 57th in season adjusted wild pitches. The positive facets of his career include one no-hitter and one Triple Crown. He had eight league leaderships in the Triple Crown categories and that coupled with his short career makes him 17th in dominance. After six declining vote percentages from the early BBWAA he was found to be famous by the 1977 Veterans Committee. It is hard to argue with his image or some of his accomplishments, but his statistics and rankings simply don't justify him.

28. Mordecai Brown – 1903-1916, WAR 45th, JAWS 45th

Brown is another unusual figure as he had fingers mangled from different events and earned the nickname "Three Fingers." He jumps way up from WAR and JAWS due to a short number of effective seasons of 12.6893. He wasn't a strikeout pitcher as he was 52nd in career strikeouts, 46th in season adjusted strikeouts and 34th in SO/BB ratio. Naturally his wins are low at 42nd place. But, he was third in ERA, fourth in ERA+, fifth in season adjusted shutouts, sixth in WHIP where he led the league three times, seventh in season adjusted wins, and eighth in won-loss percentage. He even led the league in saves four times. He won a remarkable 71.99% of his starts and is first among all in the Hall. He wasn't dominant and only saw a 17th place vote in one of two MVP considerations. After eight weak BBWAA votes he was chosen for eternal remembrance by the Veterans Committee of 1949. I can live with this one.

29. Phil Niekro – 1964-1987, WAR 10th, JAWS 14th

Pitching for 24 years until the age of 48 guarantees you longevity credit to be favorably ranked in WAR and in JAWS. Granted being a knuckleball pitcher adds to, or at least creates, an image and a unique contribution to the game, I still want to see some statistics to back up the selection, though. He was fifteenth in wins and led the league four times, but his season adjusted wins drops all the way to 61st out of 63. His won-loss percentage is 58th despite 318 wins. He only won 44.4% of his starts placing him 58th. His ERA is 53rd, 43rd in ERA+ and 46th in WHIP. His career strikeouts come in at 28th and his seasonal adjusted strikeouts check in at a stronger 20th but his SO/BB ratio slips below median to 37th. He tossed one no-hitter. He placed second in five Cy Young award votes and made five All-Star squads with a collection of four Gold Gloves. He is fifth in the history books for games started. He was not dominant with only four league leaderships in the Triple Crown categories. The BBWAA was a little hesitant, but he came in on his fifth ballot at 80.3%. This is a tough one, but he is so unique I am going to let him slide.

30. Juan Marichal – 1960-1975, WAR 39th, JAWS 30th

Some would argue that Marichal was far greater than regarded. His statistics may prove to be his torch. He was 40th in wins and that is the only ranking lower than 30. He was fourth in SO/BB ratio, seventh in WHIP, tenth in season adjusted shutouts, fifteenth in won-loss percentage and eighteenth in season adjusted strikeouts. Now for the slightly less impressive rankings. He was 21st in season adjusted wins, 23rd in ERA, 28th in career strikeouts, and 29th in ERA+. Even the less impressive are well below median. He did have one no-hitter and nine All-Star appointments. He only saw an eight for his highest vote for Cy Young and a five for his highest MVP vote. He only had three league leaderships, so dominance was not present. Up against Koufax, Drysdale and Gibson in the 1960s was bad timing. Assaults upon catchers notwithstanding, he cleared the bar in his third ballot with 83.7%.

31. Don Drysdale – 1956-1959, WAR 40th, JAWS 36th

Drysdale improves from WAR and JAWS because of a shorter career. He was well above average in strikeouts and shutouts. He was 22nd in career strikeouts but twelfth in season adjusted strikeouts and ninth in SO/BB ratio. He logged in at twelfth in season adjusted shutouts. He was 20th in WHIP, 27th in ERA and 32nd in ERA+. Continuing the cascade, he was 48th in won-loss percentage, 51st in wins, and 55th in season adjusted wins. He picked up one Cy Young Award in as many votes. He found his way to eight All-Star teams. With four league leaderships in ERA, wins and strikeouts he is nowhere near dominant. He was intimidating, though, as he led the league in hit batsmen five times. He helped his own cause with 29 homers with the bat. With ten

BBWAA votes he rose from 21% to 78%. He had great name recognition as part of the Koufax-Drysdale team and may have benefited from some coattails. I can live with it.

32. Robin Roberts – 1948-1966, WAR 16th, JAWS 21st

Roberts is the median of the 63 pitchers rated by SAWS. He is much higher in WAR and JAWS though, since he had a career on the longer side. Robert's record shows that his good years were pretty much behind him by the age of 30. He was 25th in wins but 54th in season adjusted wins and 57th in won-loss percentage. He was 16th in SO/BB ratio, and led the league five times in that category, but 25th in strikeouts and 38th in season adjusted strikeouts. He was 26th in WHIP but 48th in ERA+ and 58th in ERA. He may have led the league in wins four times, but he also led the league in losses twice. He had a good seven years in his first nine in the majors. He made seven All-Star squads and got seven looks for MVP but no wins. After that there was nothing in his awards column. He went from 56.1% to 86.9% on four ballots. In my opinion he was somewhat a flash in the pan.

33. Tim Keefe – 1880-1893, WAR 14th, JAWS 11th

Once again, we see a pitcher whose career was before the position was moved to 60'6" away from the plate. In fourteen years he accumulated over twenty effective seasons. It seems like if he was not pitching every other day he was pitching two out of every three days sometimes. He was ninth in wins but sunk a little to 24th in won-loss percentage and 31st in season adjusted wins. He was eleventh in ERA but again fell to 24th in ERA+. He was fourteenth in WHIP with four league leaderships. He was twentieth in strikeouts but 32nd in SO/BB ratio and 37th in season adjusted strikeouts. He won one Triple Crown and holds the single season consecutive win streak at nineteen. The 1936 Veterans Committee passed him over with 1.3% of the vote. The 1964 Veterans Committee correctly saw a workhorse of a different color.

34. Hoss Radbourn – 1881-1891, WAR 25th, JAWS 18th

We have another workhorse of a pitcher before the movement to a mound. He spent eleven seasons and amassed over fifteen effective seasons. He may only be 23rd in won-loss percentage but he was eighteenth in wins and came up to ninth in season adjusted wins. He also holds the all-time seasonal wins number of 59. He is also ranked fifth with 48 wins per actual season. He was fourteenth in ERA but slides to a much lower 35th in ERA+ and holds on to stay 21st in WHIP. He was clearly not a strikeout pitcher as he was 41st in strikeouts, 44th in season adjusted strikeouts and 31st in SO/BB ratio. He threw one no-hitter and one Triple Crown. He is distinctive enough to stay.

35. Gaylord Perry – 1962-1983, WAR 11th, JAWS 17th

He is ranked where he is in WAR and JAWS because those rankings look more favorably on 22 years than SAWS does. His 314 wins keep him sixteenth, but his season adjusted wins falls abysmally to 62nd while his won-loss percentage hangs on to 55th place. He is seventh in career strikeouts but falls to nineteenth in season adjusted ranking while his SO/BB matches the ranking of nineteen. There is nothing to brag about with a 36th place ERA or a 42nd place ERA+. A 29th place WHIP stays above median. He picked up two Cy Young awards and joined five All-Star teams but only came in sixth in six MVP ballots. He logged one no-hitter. The elephant in the room with Perry is his possible, or probable, use of banned substances. Substances applied to the ball rather than taken internally, that is. There are probably more suspicious events to prove that than there is proof of some players accused of PEDs. The writers may have thought so as it took three ballots and a weak 77.2% to get him in. Carew may have been his weakest ballot competition in those three years. I am not convinced he belongs.

36. Lefty Gomez – 1930-1943, WAR 57th, JAWS 61st

Although he played fourteen seasons he only had 10.5143 effective seasons. Therefore, SAWS treats him much more kindly. He was 60th in career wins but he did lead the league twice. Remarkably though, he was sixth in won-loss percentage and season adjusted wins. His ERA was 52nd but his adjusted ERA brought him up to 28th and ERA+ is not a season adjusted statistic. His WHIP is terrible and falls into the 62nd slot. His strikeouts come in 51st but his season adjusted strikeouts rise above the median to 27th and he did lead the league in strikeouts three times. His SO/BB ratio falls down to 50th but he led the league three times in that department. Overall, he led the league in the three Triple Crown categories seven times which gives him a dominance rating of eighteenth. He also had seven appointments to the All-Star squads. He did get four MVP looks and came in third in one of them. Gomez was not a great choice but he sure wasn't one of the worst either, especially for the Veterans Committee of 1972 whose immediate predecessors and successors stunk up the place with many of their decisions. The writers seem to agree that he is not Hall worthy with fifteen ballots and votes that go from .6% to 46.1%. He is not my idea of famous or great, though.

37. Jim Palmer – 1965-1984 excluding 1968, WAR 30th, JAWS 29th

An injury almost ended Palmer's career early. But he roared back after a year of rehabilitation. His best comparison category was won-loss percentage and twelfth. Next was an unusually high rank of fourteenth in season adjusted shutouts since he pitched through 1984. Tom Seaver is sixteenth in that category and he pitched through 1986 so you know Palmer is in good company. He is 29th in wins and 30th in season adjusted wins. Also above the median is his ERA at 22nd, his ERA+ at 25th and his WHIP at 28th. He begins to falter but only slightly with 31st in strikeouts, 32nd in season adjusted strikeouts and 44th in SO/BB ratio. He picked up three Cy Young awards and came in second for two more. Second in eight MVP looks can be added to his three Gold Gloves and six All-Star selections. He was not dominant with only four league leaderships in strikeouts, wins and ERA. He tossed one no-hitter. All three rankings put him close to median, but he easily came to Cooperstown with 92.6% on the first ballot. Numbers can be strange.

38. Bob Feller – 1936-1956, WAR 34th, JAWS 32nd

"Rapid Robert" drops slightly from WAR and JAWS and it is somewhat surprising to see someone of his repute to be below median in ranking. Missing three years early in his career due to military duty does not help his total numbers but most of the comparisons are averages. He was 30th in wins but led the league six times. His season adjusted wins climb to 24th and his won-loss percentage ranks 20th. With his fastball he is 19th in career strikeouts with seven league leaderships and 16th in season adjusted strikeouts. His control was not as good as his fastball was fast and his SO/BB ratio rank is 46th. His ERA sinks to 43rd but his ERA+ floats back up to 31st. His WHIP reflects his walks and drops to 53rd. He was 24th in season adjusted shutouts. He had three no-hitters, one Triple Crown and fourteen league leaderships in the Triple Crown categories pushing him up to fifth in the dominance rankings. He collected eight All-Star appointments and came in second in seven MVP votes. The Cy Young award began the year after his retirement. An easy first ballot selection at 93.8%. Image is huge part of this race.

39. Vic Willis – 1898-1910, WAR 31st, JAWS, 34th

Willis is an unknown name from the turn of the twentieth century and was a "bolt out of the blue" when he was suddenly chosen by the 1995 Veterans Committee having never received a single vote previously. Minimal is good word to describe his qualifications. His two best ranks are twelfth in ERA and eighteenth in season adjusted shutouts. He is 37th in wins and led the league in losses twice. He then shows a won-loss percentage rank of 52nd and a season adjusted wins rank of 51st. Consistency comes with his strikeout numbers at 47th in career strikeouts, 48th in season adjusted strikeouts and 49th in SO/BB ratio. His WHIP is 36th and his ERA+ is 40th. He did throw one no-hitter. Someone will have to explain this one to me.

40. Whitey Ford – 1950-1967, WAR, 48th, JAWS 50th

We have another pitcher slightly below median with fantastic image. And he has some credentials to back up that image and his election to the Hall. Even though he was 44th in career wins he vaults up to first in won-loss percentage, stays high with eighth in season adjusted wins and maintains at thirteen in season adjusted shutouts. He was seventeenth in ERA and fourteenth in ERA+ with a 38th place in WHIP. While only 37th in strikeouts and 40th in SO/BB ratio he ascends to 22nd in season adjusted strikeouts. He picked up one Cy Young award after they began in 1956. He was second in Rookie of the Year, third in one of nine MVP votes and selected to eight All-Star rosters. He has countless career World Series records from eleven trips and even took home the MVP in 1961. He came in with Mickey Mantle on his second ballot with 77.8%. As I have said before and will probably say again, the writers used to be a tough crowd. I wish they still were.

41. Tom Glavine – 1987-2008, WAR 24th, JAWS 27th

Staying healthy for 22 years allows you to acquire the above ranks in WAR and JAWS. SAWS isn't as rewarding. Although he was 20th in wins, and led the league five times, he drops slightly to 27th in season adjusted wins and to 29th in won-loss percentage. His strikeouts log in at seventeenth all-time and, again, drop to a 26th place with season adjustment. His SO/BB ratio drops below median to 42nd. His ERA at 56th and ERA+ at 39th are not impressive and neither is a 52nd place for WHIP. He picked up two Cy Young awards and two second place votes with a tenth place in one of five MVP ballots. He joined ten All-Star teams and had two Silver Sluggers. He had no dominance ranking and consequently no Triple Crowns. He did not possess a no-hitter and his post season was dismal. He came in with Greg Maddux with 91.9% of the vote. I would have been part of the 8.1% not voting for him.

42. Red Faber – 1914-1933, WAR 28th, JAWS 44th

Faber has the unusual movements of starting at 28th in WAR, dropping to 44th in JAWS and moving back up to 42nd in SAWS. None of his rankings come up to median. His closest is 33rd in wins. Next is 36th in ERA+ and 37th in ERA. Then comes 50th in WHIP, 50th in strikeouts, 52nd in season adjusted wins, 54th in won-loss percentage, 56th in season adjusted strikeouts, and 57th in SO/BB ratio. The only award available in his day was MVP and he did not scratch that surface. In sixteen ballots he went from .4 to 30.9% only to have the 1964 Veterans Committee choose him for Cooperstown. Huh?

43. Ted Lyons – 1923-1942, 1946, WAR 32nd, JAWS 35th

His rankings come up to exactly median once and then he falls precipitously in most categories. He is 32nd in wins, 50th in seasonal adjusted wins, and 61st in won-loss percentage. In strikeouts he is 59th in career strikeouts, 63rd in season adjusted strikeouts and 63rd in SA/BB ratio with the only pitcher in the Hall below one in SO/BB. That's right, he walked more batters than he struck out. His ERA is 61st and his

ERA+ is 41st while is WHIP is 58th. He had one All-Star appointment and was third in one of nine MVP looks. His Sunday drive through eleven ballots ended when he came in with 86.5% of the vote. On the same ticket Joe DiMaggio came in with 88% of the votes. Get serious BBWAA.

44. Steve Carlton – 1965-1988, WAR 19th, JAWS 16th

Just how did Carlton go from nineteenth in WAR and sixteenth in JAWS to this position? His last four years cost him dearly. Remarkably though, not all of his comparative statistics are all that good. He was tenth in wins, but his season adjusted wins comes in 47th, and his won-loss percentage comes in 43rd. His ERA checks in at 49th while his ERA+ says he is 44th. His WHIP does him no favors at 43rd. Strikeouts is where he shines. He was third in career strikeouts, sixth in season adjusted strikeouts and 28th in SO/BB ratio. He won four Cy Young awards, ten All-Star selections and one Gold Glove. In six MVP ballots he came in fifth three times. He pulled in one Triple Crown but his league leaderships in triple crown categories at eleven cause him to fall short of dominance. First ballot election with 95.6% in 1994. If I had seen these statistics in 1994 I would not have checked his box on the first ballot. But he is a Hall of Famer.

45. Jim Bunning – 1955-1971, WAR 43rd, JAWS 41st

Bunning is another strikeout pitcher. Other than strikeout statistics and WHIP he is way below median. And WAR and JAWS do not disagree. He ranks fifteenth in career strikeouts and he tops that mark with ninth in season adjusted strikeouts and continues to perform well with eleventh in SO/BB ratio. But the party is over with 45th in wins, 59th in season adjusted wins, and 51st in won-loss percentage. Then he gets very consistent with a 46th position in both ERA and ERA+. At least his WHIP is respectable at 27th. He did throw one no-hitter and one perfect game. He came in second in only one Cy Young vote and ninth in five MVP ballots. He did join seven All-Star squads. His fifteenth ballot fell short of "last ballot sympathy" votes at 74.2% and the 1996 Veterans Committee saw it in his favor. I would not have.

46. John Smoltz – 1988-2009, WAR 33rd, JAWS 43rd

Smoltz is unique because he was a great starter, suffered an injury, came back as a closer, and worked his way back to great starter. His win numbers are a little mixed, but they come in at 49th for his career, 39th in won-loss percentage and 33rd in season adjusted wins. His ERA is 50th but his ERA+ is much more respectable at 27th. His strikeouts register fourteenth while his season adjusted strikeouts register tenth and his SO/BB climb to sixth. His WHIP looks decent at 26th. He picked up one Cy Young award as a starter but no MVPs in his four ballots. He was voted into the All-Star realm eight times. As a reliever he saved 154 games and had a save percentage of 91.1% which is better than Mariano Rivera. This is distinctive in the history of the game. My first ballot vote would have been forthcoming.

47. Nolan Ryan – 1966, 1968-1993, WAR 20th, JAWS 26th

Longevity and SAWS may have taken Ryan way down, but JAWS humbled him just a little. Getting right to the heart of the matter he was first in career strikeouts and third in season adjusted strikeouts but dropping to 33rd in SO/BB ratio having led the league in walks eight times. He may rank thirteenth in wins, but he ranks 58th in season adjusted wins and 62nd in won-loss percentage. An ERA of 40th, an ERA+ of 50th and a WHIP of 44th would not get you a cup of coffee in Cooperstown. When it came to Cy Young and MVP awards he was always a bridesmaid. He did get elected to the All-Star teams eight times and has the career lead for hits per nine innings. Just for good measure you can add seven no-hitters. And he did all of this until he was 46 years old. A first ballot sure thing with 98.8% of the vote tying the then record. Sometimes calculated numbers just need to be ignored.

48. Jack Chesbro – 1899-1909, WAR 59th, JAWS 56th

SAWS may be elevating Chesbro from WAR and JAWS but that isn't saying much. He was 56th in wins and led the league twice; he was 30th in won-loss percentage and led the league twice and he was 29th in season adjusted wins. The notable win statistic came in 1904 with 41 wins which is the modern (1901 forward) record. His ERA is 15th but his ERA+ droops badly to 53rd while his WHIP stays a little higher at 22nd. He was 22nd in season adjusted shutouts. His strikeouts are 55th with a 45th ranking in season adjusted strikeouts. His SO/BB ratio came in at 38th which is still six spots below median. After four obvious rejections by the writers with a maximum of 2.2% of the votes the 1946 Old Timers Committee struck again. 41 wins is about like 61 home runs. They do not cut it.

49. Chief Bender – 1903-1917, 1925, WAR 58th, JAWS 57th

His 50th place in wins pales to the 17th place in won-loss percentage and to the 22nd place in season adjusted wins. He may have been 45th in career strikeouts but he was 31st in season adjusted strikeouts and 23rd in SO/BB ratio. He was 52nd in ERA+ but eighth in ERA and tenth in WHIP. He was fifteenth in season adjusted shutouts. After fifteen ballots ranging from .9% to 44.7% he succeeded with the 1953 Veterans Committee. There are enough flashes of brilliance to at least keep him higher than WAR and JAWS gave him. Those flashes were just not enough to light the path to Cooperstown.

50. Waite Hoyt – 1918-1938, WAR 49th, JAWS 54th

Hoyt had a great nine year run with the Yankees from 1921-1929 and that was it. Other than those years, where he had a won-loss percentage of .616, he was 80-84. In descending order, he was 45th in won-loss percentage, 49th in season adjusted wins, 50th in wins, 51st in ERA, 56th in WHIP, 57th in strikeouts, 58th in season adjusted strikeouts, 58th in SO/BB ratio, and 58th in ERA. Two MVP ballots with a tenth and 22nd place do not help his cause. In fifteen BBWAA ballots he went from .4% to 19.2% and waited for the 1969 Veterans Committee to reward him. Put him in the Yankees' Hall of Fame if you want but not the one in Cooperstown.

51. Pud Galvin – 1875, 1879-1892, WAR 21st, JAWS 23rd

Playing in an ERA where pitchers pitched about three out of every four games he amassed 24.013 effective seasons in fifteen actual ones. That is why he ranks where he does in WAR and JAWS. He played in the original National Association, the National League, the American Association and the Players League so some may not recognize all his statistics. Again, working in descending order, he was fifth in career wins and had two years of winning 46 games which is ninth all-time. He is 20th in ERA and 22nd in SO/BB. Slightly lower is his WHIP at 32nd and another drop finds his career strikeouts at 42nd. His won-loss percentage and his season adjusted wins each come in at 56th while his ERA finds the 58th slot. At the bottom is his season adjusted strikeouts in 61st place. Some good news is that he had one no-hitter and one perfect game which may have been the first. His image follows him because he was allegedly 5'6" and 190 lbs. I have seen pictures that prove that weight to be a very kind number. In any event, no votes for him were ever recorded until the 1965 Veterans Committee snatched him out of ancient history. I see him as a significant part of the game as it was back then.

52. Bob Lemon – 1941-42/1946-58, WAR 60th, JAWS 53rd

About all there is to talk about with Lemon is his statistics and they are not even that exciting. He is 53rd in wins and led the league three times. He rises quite a bit to 27th in won-loss percentage and even more to eleventh in season adjusted wins. Strikeouts are a different story. He is 54th in career whiffs, 43rd in season adjusted numbers and way down low with a 62nd place for SO/BB. His ERA comes in at 41st with a slight increase to 37th for ERA+ and his WHIP sinks to 55th. He did accomplish one no-hitter. He played on seven All-Star teams and came in fifth three times in seven MVP votes. He worked his way up to 78.6% on his fourteenth ballot. Way too plain vanilla for my taste. Nothing great or famous about this guy.

53. Mickey Welch – 1880-1892, WAR 37th, JAWS 28th

Yet another pitcher from the early years. He also pitched far more effective seasons than actual with over nineteen effective and thirteen actual. He is nineteenth in wins with 44 as a season high. But he falls dramatically to 34th in won-loss percentage and again to 45th with season adjusted wins. His strikeout figures are nothing special with a 40th position for career strikeouts, a 51st position for season adjusted strikeouts and a 48th slot for SO/BB. His ERA starts good at 16th but his ERA+ takes him down to 49th. His WHIP is slightly below median at 40th. Just like Galvin the 1973 Veterans Committee found him somewhere and anointed him. I think Galvin was enough to represent his era and this pick was just par for the course for the Veterans Committees of the late Sixties and early Seventies.

54. Don Sutton – 1966-1988, WAR 27th, JAWS 46th

Sutton may be the epitome of quantity without a lot of quality. SAWS just finished the job JAWS started. His strikeout numbers are well above average. He was sixth in career strikeouts with 3574 but never led the league in that category. He eighteenth in WHIP but led the league four times. He was fifteenth in season adjusted strikeouts and fourteenth in SO/BB ratio. He was fourteenth in wins but never led the league there either. His won-loss percentage sinks to 47th but that is higher than his 53rd rank in season adjusted wins. An ERA at 44th and an ERA+ at 56th are not high quality. From 27 years old to 32 years old he looked at four All-Stars selections, five unsuccessful Cy Young ballots and only one unsuccessful MVP vote. He crept in on his fifth ballot with 81.6%. This is one thing SAWS does well: eliminates quantity recognition.

55. Red Ruffing – 1924-1947, WAR 47th, JAWS 40th

The only comparison category above median is his 27th place in wins. His won-loss percentage sinks to 58th and his season adjusted wins comes back up to 49th. His ERA stinks at 62nd and his ERA+ isn't much better at 54th. His WHIP lives in the same neighborhood at 56th. He is 35th in strikeouts, 42nd is season adjusted strikeouts and 54th in strikeout to base on ball ratio. His heyday was solely with the Yankees because he was 231-124 with them and 37-101 otherwise. He had appearances in seven World Series and was 7-2 in ten games. He was in six All-Star games after their inception in 1933. After seventeen ballots he won the 1967 Run-Off vote. I always wonder if the Yankees helped him win or he helped the Yankees win. When in doubt, don't.

56. Eppa Rixey – 1912-1933, WAR 46th, JAWS 52nd

He was 31st in wins and only led the league once in wins but led it twice in losses. His won-loss percentage is dead last at 63rd and his season adjusted wins in not far behind at 60th. Strikeout numbers were pretty bad as well with a 53rd in career strikeouts, 62nd in season adjusted strikeouts and 55th in SO/BB ratio. His ERA was 38th and his ERA+ was 47th as was his WHIP. One MVP look got him a 22nd place. How he climbed to 52.8% on his sixteenth writers' ballot is beyond me and his selection by the 1964 Veterans Committee is even more puzzling.

57. Herb Pennock – 1912-1934, WAR 55th, JAWS 58th

His win numbers are his best, but he only comes up to median twice. His career wins are 41st while his won-loss percentage is 32nd. His season adjusted wins touch the median as well at 32nd. His ERA and ERA+ is 59th and 60th respectively. His WHIP keeps them company at 59th. His strikeouts are 56th while his season adjusted strikeouts drop to 57th and his SO/BB rises to 50th. Two MVP looks got him a third and fourth place. He did have an excellent World Series record of 5-0 with an ERA of 1.95 and a WHIP of .849. He struggled for nine ballots but climbed to 77.9%. A great candidate for the Yankees Hall of Fame again, but that is it.

58. Jack Morris – 1977-1994, WAR 54th, JAWS 59th

The selection of Morris astounds me. In addition to his low Hall of Fame rankings, he is the 161st ranked pitcher overall in JAWS and the 149th in WAR, yet he garnered 67.7% of the vote in fifteen writers' ballots and was selected by the 2018 Veterans Committee. His strikeout numbers are above median at 23rd for career strikeouts, 20th for season adjusted strikeouts but 41st in SO/BB ratio. His win numbers approach median with 34th in career wins, 40th in won-loss percentage and 34th in season adjusted wins. His ERA and ERA+ are terrible at 63rd and 61st. His WHIP comes in at 49th. His awards are moderate. Five All-Star games in eighteen years, five MVP looks with a high score of thirteenth in one of them and seven Cy Young looks where he came in third twice. He was a six-time league leader in wild pitches. He did toss one no-hitter and pitched a great seventh game in the 1991 World Series. Writers and committees must not be paying any attention to all the mathematical rankings developed to help determine who is great and who isn't.

59. Early Wynn – 1941-1963, WAR 51st, JAWS 47th

He ranks 23rd in wins with exactly 300 but he is 37th in season adjusted wins and 50th in won-loss percentage. He is 26th in career strikeouts but slips below median to 37th in season adjusted strikeouts. His SO/BB ratio is much worse at 53rd. His ERA and ERA+ are even worse coming in at 57th and 59th. His WHIP is just ahead of those rankings at 54th. In 23 seasons he captured seven All-Star appointments and eight MVP ballots with a third-place vote. He wrapped up a Cy Young award at the ripe age of 39. The writers were a little hesitant starting out with 27.9% and rising to 76% on the fourth ballot. Not even his longevity gave him much to brag about in WAR or JAWS. Not a good choice despite the 300 wins.

60. Burleigh Grimes – 1916-1934, WAR 52nd, JAWS 49th

He was 28th in wins and led the league twice while his won-loss percentage landed at 46th. His season adjusted wins came in at 44th. Strikeouts were at 49th; season adjusted strikeouts were at 55th and SO/BB was at 59th. ERA and ERA+ were almost consistent at 55th and 57th respectively. WHIP was dead last at 63rd. Four shots at MVP provided a third-place vote and he led the league twice in hit batsmen. On fourteen ballots he went from .4% to 34% and had to wait until the 1964 Veterans Committee picked him out of the crowd. I guess his nickname of "Ol' Stubblefied" and his menacing sounding name intimidated the committee.

61. Jesse Haines – 1918-1937, WAR 62nd, JAWS 63rd

He posted a 52nd for career wins and 38th for season adjusted wins. His won-loss percentage finds the 44th slot. His strikeout numbers are bottom of the barrel. Career strikeouts are 62nd, season adjusted strikeouts are 60th and SO/BB is 61st. ERA and WHIP are 60th and 61st but his ERA+ breaks away to 55th. One MVP look netted him an eighth place. He had a 3-1 record in World Series play with a 1.67 ERA. With twelve ballots and a top score of 8.3% he was forced to wait until the 1970 Veterans Committee picked up on his mediocre talents. How sad.

62. Catfish Hunter – 1965-1979, WAR 61st, JAWS 60th

His comparative statistics look better than his rankings. He was 46th in wins, 42nd in season adjusted wins and 41st in won-loss percentage. His strikeout numbers are even better with career strikeouts at 34th place, season adjusted strikeouts at 29th and SO/BB at 29th. His ERA logs in at 45th but his ERA+ takes the 62nd slot. His WHIP, though, comes in at seventeenth. He had two league leaderships in wins, WHIP and won-loss percentage. He was first, second, third and fourth in four Cy Young votes. He climbed to sixth in four MVP votes and was selected for eight All-Star teams. He threw one no-hitter and one perfect game. He pitched in six World Series with a 5-3 record. He was the first free agent as a result of a contract dispute with Charles Finley. He came to Cooperstown on his third ballot with 76.3%. This is another enigmatic situation, so I fall back on "when in doubt, don't."

63. Rube Marquard – 1908-1925, WAR 63rd. JAWS 62nd

He may have been glorious in his day and time but not with the rankings. Actually, he did look glorious, for all of three years. He did achieve some glory with his nineteen-game win streak. All in all, though, he came in 55th in career wins, 57th in season adjusted wins, and 60th in won-loss percentage. Career strikeouts registered at the 48th position while season adjusted strikeouts fared a little better at the 40th position. SO/BB almost got to the median point at 36th. His ERA came closer to median with a 34th ranking but his ERA+ dove all the way to last place. His WHIP was mediocre at 42nd. In two MVP looks he found the seventh and eighth position. But he did toss one no-hitter. Another player with thirteen ballots starting at .4% and moving to 13.95% only to be denied by the writers. The Veterans Committee of 1971 served as doorman for him to enter. Why am I not surprised it was the Veterans Committee of 1971?

THE OTHERS

Mike Mussina has struggled to increase his vote percentage (20% to 63% over five years) from the BBWAA while his SAWS of 5.817 screams to the world that Mussina would be the fifth best pitcher in the Hall of Fame under SAWS. A lot of his other numbers are good to almost great as well. His WAR of 82.9 and JAWS of 63.8 don't fare nearly as well. He is just a little on the unassuming side for me. The lack of *fame* may be the problem.

Just about everything about Roy Halladay has Hall of Fame stamped on it except his WAR (65.5) and JAWS (57.5) which are definitely middle of the room because he only played for sixteen years and 10.99 effective seasons. SAWS comes to the rescue and places him fifth overall. His ERA+ ties for sixteenth and his WHIP comes in 25th while his won-loss percentage rates him fifth in the room. So traditional comparisons show him in at least the upper portion of the room. His 18.46 season adjusted wins and his 192.52 season adjusted strikeouts both slot in as 8th in the room. He has two Cy Young awards and a post season no-hitter. He should receive serious attention.

Johan Santana has a 6.2942 SAWS which would make him the fourth greatest pitcher in the Hall of Fame under SAWS. His strikeouts per 250 innings are 245.35 right behind Sandy Koufax for fifth place. He won two Cy Young Awards and even a Triple Crown of Pitching. His ERA+ puts him ninth in the rankings. And he got all of 2.4% of the writers' vote in 2018 so his name will be discarded from future ballots. Why? It has to be the 12-season career and the writers must not think he fits the Sandy Koufax-Dizzy Dean model. Maybe not with image but he does with statistics. He sure outscores Bruce Sutter and his 12-year career.

Curt Schilling has an unbelievable SAWS to not be in the Hall of Fame. A 6.18 would rank as the fifth greatest pitcher according to SAWS. He also has 238.9 strikeouts per effective season which would also rank fifth. The rest of his numbers are good to middle of the road. He has bounced between 29% and 52% over six ballots. Schilling's problem is not with his statistics, it is with his mouth and his comments.

In his 11th year (as of April, 2018) Clayton Kershaw has a SAWS of 7.59!

RELIEF PITCHERS

THE SEASONS

	Actual	Innings	Effective
1.	Trevor Hoffman – 18	1089.1	10.893
2.	Bruce Sutter – 12	1042	10.42
3.	Rich Gossage – 22	1809.1	18.093
4.	Hoyt Wilhelm – 21	2255.2	22.552
5.	Dennis Eckersly – 25	789.2#	7.897#
6.	Rollie Fingers – 17	1701.1	17.013

THE RANKINGS

	SAWS	WAR	JAWS
1.	Trevor Hoffman – 2.58	Wilhelm – 50.1	Wilhelm – 36.9
2.	Bruce Sutter – 2.36	Gossage – 41.9	Gossage – 36.7
3.	Rich Gossage – 2.32	Hoffman – 28.1	Sutter – 24.3
4.	Hoyt Wilhelm – 2.22	Fingers – 25.1	Hoffman – 23.7
5.	Dennis Eckersly – 2.15#	Sutter – 24.6	Fingers – 22.3
6.	Rollie Fingers – 1.48	Eckersley – 17#	Eckersley – 16.7#

- Figures for Eckersley are only from his numbers as a reliever and not as a starter.

It is obvious to the author that the above rankings are not meaningful for choosing a Hall of Fame reliever or in comparison to starting pitchers. Other categories should be evaluated for qualification to the Hall of Fame. See below.

THE COMPARISONS

	Saves	Save %	Saves/Season	ERA+
1.	Hoffman – 601	Hoffman – 88.8	Hoffman – 55.17	Wilhelm – 147
2.	Eckersley – 390	Eckersley – 84.6	Eckersley – 49.39	Hoffman – 141
3.	Fingers – 341	Wilhelm – 76	Sutter – 28.79	Sutter – 136
4.	Gossage – 310	Fingers – 75.8	Fingers – 20.04	Gossage – 126
5.	Sutter – 300	Sutter – 74.8	Gossage – 17.13	Fingers – 120
6.	Wilhelm – 228	Gossage – 73.5	Wilhelm – 10.09	Eckersley – 116

	SO/Season	SO/BB Ratio	WHIP
1.	Hoffman – 104.4	Hoffman – 3.69	Hoffman – 1.058
2.	Gossage – 83.3	Eckersley – 3.25	Wilhelm – 1.125
3.	Sutter – 82.2	Sutter – 2.79	Sutter – 1.140

4. Fingers – 76.7	Fingers – 2.60	Fingers – 1.156
5. Eckersley – 73.3	Wilhelm – 2.07	Eckersley – 1.161
6. Wilhelm – 71.1	Gossage – 2.05	Gossage – 1.232

OBSERVATIONS AND COMMENTARY

Hoffman is clearly the winner under SAWS and all categories but ERA+ and his 141 figure, although second among relief pitchers would rank sixth among all HOF starting pitchers. I would leave Hoffman in and delete the others.

THE OTHERS

Mariano Rivera will soon become the Babe Ruth of relief pitchers. His SAWS will be 4.386. His ERA+ is 205 while his strikeout to walk ratio is 4.10 and his WHIP is 1.00. He will also lead in total saves with 652 with a save percentage of 89.1. He will make it even more difficult for Lee Smith, John Franco and Billy Wagner to ever get in – not that they should.

POSITION PLAYERS CONSOLIDATIONS

THE RANKINGS (WAR and JAWS reflect rank only.)

SAWS	WAR	JAWS
1. Babe Ruth – 11.61	1	1
2. Ted Williams – 9.84	10	9
3. Rogers Hornsby – 9.79	8	5
4. Willie Mays – 9.09	2	2
5. Lou Gehrig – 8.67	11	11
6. Ty Cobb – 8.47	3	3
7. Mickey Mantle – 8.37	13	12
8. Tris Speaker – 8.20	5	6
9. Dan Brouthers – 7.92	35	36
10. Jackie Robinson – 7.90	83	62
11. Honus Wagner – 7.86	6	7
12. Mike Schmidt – 7.67	17	15
13. Stan Musial – 7.64	7	8
14. Eddie Collins – 7.56	9	10
15. Joe DiMaggio – 7.53	37	33
16. Hank Aaron – 7.46	4	4
17. Jimmie Foxx – 7.40	21	19
18. Nap Lajoie – 7.25	15	14
19. Johnny Mize – 7.20	50	43
20. Arky Vaughn – 7.07	47	40
21. Mel Ott – 6.97	14	16
22. Roger Connor – 6.961	30	31
23. Hank Greenberg – 6.959	89	80
24. Eddie Mathews – 6.94	19	22
25. Joe Morgan – 6.75	18	18
26. Roberto Clemente – 6.72	23	23
27. Billy Hamilton – 6.67	78	78
28. Frank Baker – 6.60	80	69
29. Frank Robinson – 6.57	16	17
30. Lou Boudreau – 6.53	79	65
31. Wade Boggs – 6.52	26	24
32. Rickey Henderson – 6.48	12	13
33. Mickey Cochrane – 6.32	110	105
34. Ed Delahanty – 6.27	57	49
35. Jeff Bagwell – 6.26	34	35
36. Joe Gordon – 6.24	92	83
37. Frank Chance – 6.23	129	124

38. Johnny Bench – 6.19	41	41
39. Cap Anson – 6.14	24	28
40. Buck Ewing – 6.12	123	129
41. Charlie Gehringer – 6.04	33	30
42. Duke Snider – 6.03	70	51
43. George Davis – 6.01	29	34
44. Rod Carew – 5.9808	32	32
45. Elmer Flick – 5.978	106	94
46. Chipper Jones – 5.95	28	29
47. Harry Heilmann – 5.84	49	45
48. Barry Larkin – 5.8320	54	61
49. Larry Doby – 5.830	117	104
50. Al Kaline – 5.829	25	26
51. Ralph Kiner – 5.77	118	96
52. Mike Piazza – 5.71	86	84
53. Bill Dickey – 5.66	93	103
54. Bill Terry – 5.61	97	90
55. Hughie Jennings – 5.589	139	123
56. Joe Cronin – 5.586	68	67
57. Ken Griffey – 5.52	31	27
58. George Brett – 5.51	27	25
59. Gary Carter – 5.40	56	48
60. Ryne Sandberg – 5.38	64	55
61. Al Simmons – 5.36	60	58
62. Alan Trammell – 5.35	51	52
63. Cal Ripken – 5.34	22	20
64. Roger Bresnahan – 5.33	141	143
65. Ernie Lombardi – 5.2928	126	140
66. Frank Thomas – 5.2915	45	47
67. Ron Santo – 5.2677	52	38
68. Sam Thompson – 5.266	132	130
69. Yogi Berra – 5.25	87	89
70. Luke Appling – 5.24	43	50
71. Earle Combs – 5.21	138	133
72. Pee Wee Reese – 5.20	69	77
73. Frankie Frisch – 5.18	53	57
74. Hack Wilson – 5.1701	143	136
75. Paul Waner – 5.166	48	54
76. Ozzie Smith – 5.15	39	44

77. Fred Clarke – 5.14	65	82
78. Jimmy Collins – 5.12	105	97
79. Tim Raines – 5.11	58	64
80. Sam Crawford – 5.10	42	56
81. Kirby Puckett – 5.08	113	106
82. Gabby Hartnett – 5.07	103	119
83. Richie Ashburn – 5.0608	76	73
84. Jim Thome – 5.0567	46	59
85. Goose Goslin – 5.0444	71	71
86. Tony Gwynn – 5.0416	59	66
87. Earl Averill - 5.0211	121	115
88. Jesse Burkett – 5.0152	81	87
89. Bobby Wallace – 4.99	54	63
90. Joe Medwick – 4.98	94	92
91. Willie McCovey – 4.97	74	70
92. Carl Yastrzemski – 4.96	20	21
93. King Kelly – 4.937	133	135
94. Joe Tinker – 4.9347	107	112
95. Tony Lazzeri – 4.9141	116	116
96. Roy Campanella – 4.9085	149	144
97. Deacon White – 4.8691	128	142
98. Carlton Fisk – 4.8672	63	79
99. Roberto Alomar – 4.86	67	68
100. Ivan Rodriguez – 4.77	62	72
101. Joe Sewell – 4.75	102	99
102. Joe Kelley – 4.74	114	110
103. Billy Herman – 4.73	96	108
104. Vladimir Guerrero – 4.72	88	86
105. Paul Molitor – 4.68	40	53
106. Willie Stargell – 4.67	90	91
107. Reggie Jackson – 4.606	44	42
108. Enos Slaughter – 4.600	95	100
109. Chuck Klein – 4.59	135	127
110. Bobby Doerr – 4.58	112	109
111. Ernie Banks – 4.57	66	46
112. Brooks Robinson – 4.56	36	39
113. Robin Yount – 4.553	38	37
114. Travis Jackson – 4.547	134	128
115. Harmon Killebrew – 4.52	84	88

116. Johnny Evers – 4.51	122	125
117. Ross Youngs – 4.42	150	147
118. George Sisler – 4.40	101	85
119. Andre Dawson – 4.38	73	75
120. Willie Keeler – 4.37	98	102
121. Phil Rizzuto – 4.36	142	137
122. Billy Williams – 4.35	77	81
123. KiKi Cuyler – 4.31	125	122
124. Jake Beckley – 4.30	82	98
125. Dave Bancroft – 4.27	120	114
126. Zack Wheat – 4.259	85	93
127. Chick Hafey – 4.255	151	151
128. Jim O'Rourke – 4.24	111	134
129. Hugh Duffy – 4.16	136	139
130. Heine Manush – 4.11	127	126
131. Bid McPhee – 4.09	109	121
132. Orlando Cepeda – 4.08	115	117
133. Craig Biggio – 4.011	72	76
134. Edd Rousch – 4.008	131	132
135. Sam Rice – 3.90	108	120
136. Harry Hooper – 3.88	104	95
137. Eddie Murray – 3.800	61	74
138. Jim Rice – 3.799	124	118
139. Dave Winfield – 3.70	75	60
140. Luis Aparicio – 3.63	92	107
141. George Kell – 3.622	144	145
142. Tony Perez – 3.6206	100	101
143. Max Carey – 3.6	99	111
144. John M Ward – 3.58	148	150
145. Nellie Fox – 3.52	119	113
146. Fred Lindstrom – 3.45	154	152
147. Red Schoendienst – 3.23	145	138
148. Pie Traynor – 3.14	146	149
149. Jim Bottomley – 3.10	147	146
150. Lou Brock – 3.07	130	131
151. Bill Mazeroski – 2.90	145	148
152. Ray Schalk – 2.89	153	153
153. Rick Ferrell – 2.87	152	154
154. High Pockets Kelly – 2.70	155	155

155. Rabbit Maranville – 2.67	137	141
156. Lloyd Waner – 2.27	156	156
157. Tommy McCarthy – 2.09	157	157

OBSERVATIONS AND COMMENTARY

Noticeable moves up from JAWS to SAWS:

B. Ewing goes from 129th to 40th

F. Chance goes from 124th to 37th

R. Bresnahan goes from 113th to 64th

E. Lombardi goes from 140th to 65th

M. Cochrane goes from 105th to 33rd

H. Jennings goes from 113th to 64th

H. Greenberg goes from 80th to 23rd

S. Thompson goes from 130th to 68th

E. Combs goes from 133rd to 71st

H. Wilson goes from 136th to 74th

L. Doby goes from 104th to 49th

B. Hamilton goes from 78th to 27th

B. Dickey goes from 103rd to 53rd

E. Flick goes from 94th to 45th

R. Cmpanella goes from 144th to 96th

J. Gordon goes from 83rd to 36th

R. Kiner goes from 96th to 51st

D. White goes from 142nd to 97th

J. Robinson goes from 62nd to 10th

K. Kelly goes from 135th to 93rd

F. Baker goes from 69th to 28th

G. Hartnett goes from 119th to 37th

L. Boudreau goes from 65th to 30th

K. Puckett goes from 106th to 81st

M. Piazza goes from 84th to 52nd

R. Youngs goes from 147th to 117th

E. Averill goes from 115th to 87th

D. Brouthers goes from 36th to 9th

J. Mize goes from 43rd to 19th

A. Vaughn goes from 40th to 20th

J. DiMaggio goes from 33rd to 15th

T. Williams goes from 9th to 2nd

L. Gehrig goes from 11th to 5th

Noticeable moves down from JAWS to SAWS:

D. Winfield goes from 60th to 139th

R. Yount goes from 37th to 113th

B. Robinson goes from 39th to 112th

C. Ystrzemski goes from 21st to 92nd

E. Banks goes from 46th to 111th

R. Jackson goes from 42nd to 107th

C. Biggio goes from 76th to 133rd

P. Molitor goes from 53rd to 105th

A. Dawson goes from 75th to 119th

C. Ripken goes from 20th to 63rd

B. Williams goes from 81st to 122nd

H. Hooper goes from 96th to 136th

Z. Wheat goes from 93rd to 126th

G. Sisler goes from 85th to 118th

O. Smith goes from 44th to 76th

R. Alomar goes from 68th to 99th

J. Thome goes from 59th to 84th

G. Brett goes from 25th to 58th

K. Griffey goes from 27th to 57th

R. Santo goes from 38th to 67th

I. Rodriguez goes from 72nd to 100th

S. Crawford goes from 56th to 80th

A. Kaline goes from 26th to 50th

T. Gwynn goes from 66th to 86th

R. Henderson goes from 13th to 32nd

C. Jones goes from 29th to 46th

H. Aaron goes from 4th to 16th

F. Robinson goes from 17th to 29th

As noted in the introduction certain players were buoyed by SAWS to the positions some may argue they do not deserve. Others may take the opposite argument that SAWS improperly demotes players. Jackie Robinson is now the tenth greatest player in the game. I can support that conclusion. It has long since been believed that in order to break the racial barriers of the past that the African-American had to be better than the white man to succeed. I think Jackie Robinson was more than just the first to play in the majors; he was one of the greatest players separate from the color of his skin.

Dan Brouthers may have been the most dominant player of the 19th century but he has never received the recognition he deserves. Even a serious baseball fan may not know anything about him. Maybe SAWS will honor him.

I am sure no one argued too much about Ted Williams, Lou Gehrig and Mickey Mantle moving up the ladder.

Hank Greenberg is no longer penalized for serving his country and Ralph Kiner still has respect even though pain pushed him out of the game.

Hughie Jennings is a name some have scorned but sixth position as a shortstop and 55th overall is a truly great player.

Mickey Cochrane makes the most dramatic leap to take over a No.1 spot as catcher. Is it a violation of all protocol to move Bench from that position?

I think Joe DiMaggio deserves a rank higher than what was an actual tie with George Davis at 33/34 under JAWS. No ranking system is perfect, but he is infinitely better than Ken Griffey.

Granted there is nothing anyone can do about Tommy McCarthy, Lloyd Waner and High Pockets Kelly. At least all three computations agree on something. McCarthy was ranked 132nd overall as a right fielder; Waner was 115th as a centerfielder; and Kelly was ranked 89th as a first-basemen. But what about Lou Brock and Bill Mazeroski?

Should Carl Yastrzemski and Brooks Robinson be 92nd and 112th respectively?

You make the call.

THE CREAM OF THE SEASON ADJUSTED CROP

Season Adjusted Home Runs – Cutoff at 30

1. Babe Ruth – 51.14
2. Ralph Kiner – 43.13
3. Harmon Killebrew – 42.91
4. Jim Thome – 42.45
5. Ted Williams – 41.64
6. Ken Griffey – 41.51
7. Mike Piazza – 41.03
8. Jimmie Foxx – 40.99
9. Mickey Mantle – 40.67
10. Willie McCovey – 40.20
11. Hank Greenberg – 39.99
12. Hank Aaron – 39.39
13. Mike Schmidt – 39.31
14. Willie Stargell – 38.57
15. Willie Mays – 38.38
16. Lou Gehrig – 38.03
17. Frank Thomas – 37.31
18. Duke Snider – 36.93
19. Eddie Mathews – 36.80
20. Johnny Mize – 36.41
21. Frank Robinson – 35.86
22. Vladimir Guerrero – 35.69
23. Jeff Bagwell – 35.16
24. Reggie Jackson – 35.04
25. Roy Campanella – 34.83
26. Joe DiMaggio – 34.82
27. Ernie Banks – 34.67
28. Mel Ott – 33.03
29. Chipper Jones – 32.7
30. Hack Wilson – 32.43
31. Johnny Bench – 32.02
32. Yogi Berra – 31.65
33. Chuck Klein – 31.59
34. Orlando Cepeda – 30.81

Season Adjusted Runs Batted In – Cutoff at 120

1. Babe Ruth – 158.6
2. Sam Thompson – 154.8
3. Lou Gehrig – 153.93
4. Hank Greenberg – 153.92
5. Joe DiMaggio – 148.3
6. Jimmie Foxx – 147.5
7. Ted Williams – 146.6
8. Jesse Burkett – 142.3
9. Hack Wilson – 141.3
10. Cap Anson – 135.7
11. Johnny Mize – 135.6
12. Ed Delahanty – 131.8
13. Mike Piazza – 128.3
14. Chuck Klein – 126.45
15. Yogi Berra – 126.42
16. Hugh Duffy – 125.6
17. Jim Bottomley – 125.1
18. Willie Stargell – 125.0
19. Harry Heilmann – 124.5
20. Joe Medwick – 123.8
21. Roy Campanella – 123.2
22. Goose Goslin – 123.0
23. Bill Dickey – 122.6
24. Rogers Hornsby – 122.06
25. Frank Thomas – 122.01
26. Earl Averill – 121.8
27. Dan Brouthers – 121.3
28. Ken Griffey – 120.98
29. Duke Snider – 120.96
30. Mel Ott – 120.3

Season Adjusted Runs Scored – Cutoff at 130

Runs scored clearly favor the 19th century players who reached base and scored on a much larger number of errors due to the lack of gloves or gloves as we know them now.

1. Billy Hamilton – 178.5
2. Babe Ruth – 155.71
3. King Kelly – 152.7
4. Hugh Duffy – 149.9
5. Sam Thompson – 149.7
6. Lou Gehrig – 148.7
7. Ted Williams – 146.6
8. Earle Combs – 145.5
9. Buck Ewing – 144.8
10. Dan Brouthers – 142.5
11. Jesse Burkett – 142.3
12. Willie Keeler – 138.8
13. Tommy McCarthy – 137.6
14. Joe DiMaggio – 134.1
15. Roger Connor – 133.8
16. Charlie Gehringer – 132.9
17. Ed Delahanty – 131.8
18. Jimmie Foxx – 131.7
19. Hughie Jennings – 131.01
20. Bid McPhee – 130.8
21. Cap Anson – 130.7

Season Adjusted Runs Created – Cutoff at 130

Runs are what drives wins and wins are what drives Wins Above Replacement. You can easily see the importance.

1. Babe Ruth – 194.66
2. Ted Williams – 190.4
3. Lou Gehrig – 172.3
4. Jimmie Foxx – 163.51

5. Rogers Hornsby – 157.57
6. Hank Greenberg – 156.09
7. Mickey Mantle – 154.34
8. Stan Musial – 153.37
9. Joe DiMaggio – 151.35
10. Johnny Mize – 145.34
11. Dan Brouthers – 143.95
12. Chuck Klein – 143.61
13. Frank Thomas – 143.35
14. Ed Delahanty – 141.41
15. Ty Cobb – 141.10
16. Jeff Bagwell – 140.02
17. Al Simmons – 139.18
18. Sam Thompson – 139.06
19. Earl Averill – 138.39
20. Jim Thome – 138.10
21. Willie Mays – 137.7
22. Chipper Jones – 137.29
23. Hack Wilson – 136.9
24. Mel Ott – 134.84
25. Harry Heilmann – 134.44
26. Duke Snider – 134.02
27. Ralph Kiner – 133.70
28. Hank Aaron – 133.14
29. Bill Terry – 132.59
30. Mike Piazza – 132.42
31. Tris Speaker – 131.63
32. Ken Griffey – 131.39

<u>Season Adjusted League Leaders – Cutoff at 1.00 – Dominance Ranking</u>

This is a combination of longevity and seasonal performance which can indicate dominance. I took the six major categories of hitting as follows: batting average, on base percentage, slugging percentage, on base plus slugging, home runs and runs batted in and then I added up how many times each of the HOF hitters won those categories in their career. I then divided the league leaderships by effective seasons and stopped at quotient of one.

1. Babe Ruth – 3.868
2. Ted Williams – 3.597
3. Rogers Hornsby – 3.236
4. Dan Brouthers – 2.879
5. Ty Cobb – 2.355
6. Honus Wagner – 1.800
7. Mike Schmidt – 1.793
8. Jimmie Foxx – 1.688
9. Stan Musial – 1.676
10. Ralph Kiner – 1.636
11. Ed Delahanty – 1.618
12. Johnny Mize – 1.521
13. Lou Gehrig – 1.466
14. Mickey Mantle – 1.442
15. Chuck Klein – 1.369
16. Cap Anson – 1.177
17. Nap Lajoie – 1.147
18. Sam Thompson – 1.067
19. Hack Wilson – 1.063

<u>Season Adjusted Offensive WAR – Cutoff at 6.5 oWAR</u>

1. Babe Ruth – 11.05
2. Ted Williams – 10.10
3. Rogers Hornsby – 9.38
4. Ty Cobb – 8.98
5. Mickey Mantle – 8.83
6. Lou Gehrig – 8.66
7. Dan Brothers – 8.18
8. Willie Mays – 7.95
9. Tris Speaker – 7.60
10. Stan Musial – 7.47
11. Honus Wagner – 7.34
12. Eddie Collins – 7.31

13. Jimmie Foxx – 7.23
14. Joe DiMaggio – 7.08
15. Joe Morgan – 7.01
16. Jackie Robinson – 6.98
17. Hank Aaron – 6.91
18. Arky Vaughn – 6.83
19. Eddie Mathews – 6.79
20. Hank Greenberg – 6.77
21. Mel Ott – 6.7
22. Nap Lajoie – 6.63
23. Mike Schmidt – 6.58
24. Roger Connor – 6.56
25. Frank Robinson – 6.55
26. Billy Hamilton – 6.50

Season Adjusted Defensive WAR – Cutoff at 1.25 dWAR

1. Joe Tinker – 3.20
2. Ozzie Smith – 2.96
3. Phil Rizzuto – 2.45
4. Joe Gordon – 2.44
5. Lou Boudreau – 2.43
6. Travis Jackson – 2.30
7. Brooks Robinson – 2.27
8. Luis Aparicio – 2.07
9. Dave Bancroft – 2.07
10. Ivan Rodriguez – 2.06
11. Bobby Wallace – 2.04
12. Pee Wee Reese – 2.01
13. Gary Carter – 2.01
14. Cal Ripken – 1.99
15. Rabbit Maranville – 1.92
16. Bill Mazeroski – 1.91
17. Alan Trammell – 1.72
18. George Davis – 1.70
19. Johnny Bench – 1.62
20. Jim Collins – 1.61
21. Frankie Frisch – 1.59
22. Nellie Fox – 1.51
23. Johnny Evers – 1.46
24. Ray Schalk – 1.39
25. Luke Appling – 1.34
26. Mike Schmidt – 1.31
27. Jackie Robinson – 1.30
28. Honus Wagner – 1.28
29. Red Schoendienst – 1.27
30. Bid McPhee – 1.26

ADDITIONAL PITCHING COMPARISONS

Season Adjusted League Leaderships – Starting Pitchers – Cutoff at .5000 – Dominance Ranking

To calculate this seasonal adjustment for dominance for starting pitchers I added all the league leaderships the pitchers had in ERA, wins and strikeouts which are the three prongs of the Triple Crown. I then divided that total by effective seasons and stopped at a quotient of .500

1. Sandy Koufax – 1.2907
2. Lefty Grove – 1.2688
3. Dazzy Vance – 1.0112
4. Walter Johnson - .9722
5. Bob Feller - .9146
6. Randy Johnson - .8464
7. Pete Alexander - .8189
8. Dizzy Dean - .7625
9. Rube Waddell - .7599
10. Pedro Martinez - .7598
11. Warren Spahn - .7432
12. Christy Mathewson - .7309
13. Lefty Gomez - .7005
14. Hal Newhouser - .6682

15. Nolan Ryan - .6034
16. Tom Seaver - .5750
17. Amos Rusie - .5293
18. Joe McGinnity - .5244

% Wins per Games Started – Starting Pitchers – Not Season Adjusted

As a pure afterthought I have included this ranking. This is something I have never seen or heard of before and wondered why not. Obviously, the pitchers of earlier years have a far greater percentage of wins per start than more recent pitchers. The problem I have is explaining the phenomenon. I know that pitchers nowadays do not complete nearly as many games as starting pitchers are now expected to pitch a maximum of seven innings and yield the mound to a set-up man who yields to a closer. Starting pitchers are pulled even faster than seven innings when there is the slightest hint of a problem and don't get as many decisions whereas it seems that 75-100 years ago pitchers had to work their way out of a jam and completed more games and got more wins. I wonder if the whole concept of relief pitchers misses a great chance to win games. Would you take a pitcher out of a game if there is a 70% chance of him winning? If you pull him quickly do you even know what his true chances of winning are? Why would you want a pitcher that wins less than half of their starts? I am not sure how to interpret or use this. What follows is one of the categories of statistics I adjusted to effective seasons but rarely used so I have separated it from the rest.

1. Mordecai Brown – 71.99
2. Christy Mathewson – 67.57
3. Lefty Grove – 65.65
4. Dizzy Dean – 65.22
5. Joe McGinnity – 64.57
6. Hoss Radbourn – 64.55
7. Kid Nichols – 64.23
8. Chief Bender – 63.47
9. John Clarkson – 63.32
10. Cy Young – 62.70
11. Walter Johnson – 62.61
12. Pete Alexander – 62.17
13. Ed Walsh – 61.90
14. Ed Plank – 61.63
15. Addie Joss – 61.54
16. Jack Chesbro – 59.64
17. Bob Lemon – 59.14
18. Lefty Gomez – 59.06
19. Carl Hubbell – 58.43
20. Amos Rusie – 57.61
21. Tim Keefe – 57.58
22. Herb Pennock – 57.52
23. Rube Waddell – 56.76
24. Dazzy Vance – 56.45
25. Mickey Welch – 55.92
26. Stan Coveleski – 55.84
27. Waite Hoyt – 55.76
28. Hal Newhouser – 55.35
29. Bob Feller – 54.96
30. Warren Spahn – 54.59
31. Burleigh Grimes – 54.33
32. Jesse Haines – 54.26
33. Whitey Ford – 53.88
34. Ted Lyons – 53.72
35. Pedro Martinez – 53.55
36. Juan Marichal – 53.17
37. Pud Galvin – 53.05
38. Vic Willis – 52.89
39. Red Faber – 52.59
40. Sandy Koufax – 52.55
41. Bob Gibson – 52.07
42. Jim Palmer – 51.44

43. Red Ruffing – 50.74
44. Randy Johnson – 50.25
45. Rube Marquard – 49.26
46. Early Wynn – 49.10
47. Jack Morris – 48.20
48. Tom Seaver – 48.07
49. Eppa Rixey – 48.01
50. Greg Maddux – 47.97
51. Fergie Jenkins – 47.81
52. Catfish Hunter – 47.06
53. Robin Roberts – 46.96
54. Steve Carlton – 46.40
55. Gaylord Perry – 45.51
56. Don Drysdale – 44.95
57. Tom Glavine – 44.72
58. Phil Niekro – 44.41
59. John Smoltz – 44.28
60. Jim Bunning – 43.16
61. Don Sutton – 42.86
62. Nolan Ryan – 41.91
63. Bert Blyleven – 41.90

What follows is one of the categories of statistics I adjusted to effective seasons but rarely used so I have separated it from the rest. I found No. 62 interesting.

Season Adjusted Wild Pitches

1. Dizzy Dean – 1.5249
2. Robin Roberts – 1.7596
3. Pete Alexander – 1.8304
4. Waite Hoyt – 2.5915
5. Joe McGinnity – 2.6218
6. Red Ruffing – 2.6473
7. Early Wynn – 2.7936
8. Stan Coveleski – 2.9391
9. Addie Joss – 3.0082
10. Dazzy Vance – 3.1180
11. Jim Bunning – 3.1247
12. Lefty Grove – 3.2335
13. Ted Lyons – 3.3045
14. Fergie Jenkins – 3.4439
15. Greg Maddux – 3.4942
16. Catfish Hunter – 3.5514
17. Carl Hubbell – 3.6095
18. Tom Glavine – 3.6820
19. Juan Marichal – 3.6960
20. Lefty Gomez – 3.9026
21. Warren Spahn – 4.0131
22. Jesse Haines – 4.2853
23. Bob Feller – 4.5074
24. Herb Pennock – 4.5497
25. Mordecai Brown – 4.8072
26. Ed Plank – 4.8936
27. Don Sutton – 5.3007
28. Cy Young – 5.3018
29. Jack Chesbro – 5.3510
30. Jim Palmer – 5.3825
31. Eppa Rixey – 5.3953
32. Hal Newhouser – 5.4293
33. Pedro Martinez – 5.4922
34. Burleigh Grimes – 5.5024
35. Bob Lemon – 5.5263
36. Bert Blyleven – 5.7344
37. Vic Willis – 5.8809
38. Whitey Ford – 5.9142
39. Don Drysdale – 5.9742
40. Christy Mathewson – 6.0037
41. Rube Marquard – 6.1240
42. Rube Waddell – 6.2477
43. Ed Walsh – 6.4096
44. Walter Johnson – 6.5096
45. Chief Bender – 6.5462
46. Tom Seaver – 6.5858
47. Randy Johnson – 6.5896
48. Red Faber – 6.7904
49. Bob Gibson – 6.9510
50. Gaylord Perry – 7.4766

51. Kid Nichols – 8.3383
52. John Smoltz – 8.7586
53. Steve Carlton – 8.7683
54. Pud Galvin – 9.2033
55. Sandy Koufax – 9.3576
56. John Clarkson – 10.0301
57. Amos Rusie – 10.1226
58. Phil Niekro – 10.4552
59. Tim Keefe – 11.8820
60. Hoss Radbourn – 12.7858
61. Nolan Ryan – 12.8574
62. Jack Morris – 13.4676
63. Mickey Welch – 14.2649

INDEX

INDEX

M

N

O

P

R

S

T

V

W

Y

Printed in the United States
By Bookmasters